Populations of the
SAARC Countries
Bio-cultural Perspectives

Populations of the SAARC Countries
Bio-cultural Perspectives

Edited by
Jayanta Sarkar
G.C. Ghosh

STERLING PUBLISHERS PRIVATE LIMITED

> **DEDICATED**
> to
> *Dr Jyotirmoy Chakraborty*

STERLING PUBLISHERS PRIVATE LIMITED
A-59 Okhla Industrial Area, Phase-II, New Delhi-110020.
Tel: 26386209, 26387070; Fax: 91-11-26383788
E-mail: ghai@nde.vsnl.net.in
www.sterlingpublishers.com

Populations of the SAARC Countries : Bio-cultural Perspectives
© 2003, The Director, Anthropological Survey of India
ISBN 81 207 2562 x

Reprint 2004

All rights are reserved. No part of this publication may be reproduced, stored in a retrieval system or transmitted, in any form or by any means, mechanical, photocopying, recording or otherwise, without prior written permission of the original publisher.

PRINTED IN INDIA

Published by Sterling Publishers Pvt. Ltd., New Delhi-110 020.
Laserset at Vikas Compographics, New Delhi-110020.
Printed at : Sai Early Learners (P) Ltd.

Foreward

The South Asian Association for Regional Cooperation (SAARC) encompasses seven countries of a large landmass containing one-fifth of the total global population. After the formation of the SAARC in August 1980, several publications have been brought out by many organisations, which by and large deal with issues like economy, politics, administration and so on. The present volume *Populations of the SAARC Countries : Bio-cultural Perspectives* is first of its kind which discusses, in depth, the biological and cultural affinities/linkages of the populations of these countries. The biological affinities of the populations in respect of these countries have been traced back from the perhistoric to the contemporary period while the cultural linkages with special reference to trade, religion, art, architecture etc have been documented from ancient to the medieval period of the region. The formation of the SAARC was the fruit of intense political initiative in response to the recognition that there were deep-cultural linkages between the member countries. However, the form it assumed stresses more on economic and developmental aspects in which the wealth of respective member countries has often played a controlling role, while the bio-cultural linkages are subsumed. It is because of this that we find interest in such things surfacing at the time of the conferences of the SAARC during which economic exchange makes more headlines. It behoves on the member countries to focus attention on the linkages that have existed since times immemorial so that initiatives other than political may be explored. More and more studies on the various aspects may reveal the similarities in mindset, lifestyle and aspirations of people and go a long way in forging, enduring and permeating regional cooperation.

Populations of the SAARC Countries : Bio-cultural Perspectives, based on the review of literature published in several languages has comprehensively presented the nature and extent of affinities/ linkages that the people of these countries once had and are still maintaining in many areas. This is an area of research which hitherto drew minimum attention of scholars. Readers of this volume will get a picture of the biological and cultural relations of the people of the SAARC countries and hopefully will provide feedbacks to the interested scholars and also to those who are actively involved in bringing together the people of all the seven SAARC nations.

I am sure that the volume comprising three articles, besides the introductory note by the editors and a discussion on the imprtant issues that emerged from the review of the bio-cultural relations, will have a large readership, particularly among the people of the SAARC countries.

The Anthropological Survey of India takes pride in the publication of this volume and I take this opportunity to congratulate the editors and the contributors for giving shape to this volume.

R.K. Bhattacharya
Director
Anthropological Survey of India

Preface

South Asian Association for Regional Cooperation (SAARC) was formed in August 1980. This necessitated dissemination of knowledge all over the globe in respect of the life and culture of the people of its member nations in order to build up a mass-based stable relation so that the common people could appreciate each others' cultural heritage, removing many misconceptions. There is no dearth of literature, specially on the contemporary economic and political situations of the SAARC countries. However, unfortunately there hardly exists any anthropological literature, which comprehensively put forth the biological affinities and cultural relations of the people of these nations since early period of history and prehistory.

The present book, *Populations of the SAARC Countries: Biocultural Perspectives*, is an attempt to bring together all such fragmented information in various forms, which are available in scattered manner in published materials in different languages. An anthropological analysis and interpretation of such information has reaffirmed the presence of cultural linkages and biological affiliation even in the distant past.

A number of issues delineated in this work are expected to inspire scholars and academicians in searching many more unknown realms of biological and cultural linkages of the populations of the SAARC nations. The editors are thankful to Sterling Publishers Private Limited who has shown interest in bringing out this publication.

Editors

Contents

Foreword   v
Preface   vii
Introduction
    G.C. Ghosh and J.K. Sarkar   1

Part-I
Biological Perspectives

1. Biological Relationship of the Populations of Sri Lanka, Maldives and Pakistan with Those of India
   Chumki Piplai   9

2. Biological Affinities of the Populations of Nepal, Bhutan and Bangladesh with Those of India
   J.M. Sarkar   39

Part-II
Cultural Perspectives

3. Cultural Linkages Among the People of India, Sri Lanka, Nepal, Bhutan and Maldives
   Jyotirmoy Chakraborty and Rabiranjan Biswas   55

4. Epilogue
   J.K. Sarkar and G.C. Ghosh   126
   References   143
   About the Contributors   159

Introduction

G.C. Ghosh and J.K. Sarkar

South Asia, consisting of India, Pakistan, Bangladesh, Sri Lanka, Maldives, Bhutan and Nepal is a large landmass containing one fifth of the total global population. This region is enormously rich in terms of biotic and abiotic resources. It has a huge forest coverage and endless source of minerals coupled with viable human resource endowment. In spite of all the basic components and inherent natural wealth, progress and development of this region suffer a glaring set back. This is partly because of the colonial legacy of subjugation under which the area had to pass through. The urge for consorted effort for the benefit of the economically weak and the underdeveloped human souls mooted the concept towards formation of a common forum, 'South Asian Association for Regional Cooperation' (SAARC) in August 1980. This idea received intellectual nourishment on account of common ethnic, social, cultural and historical background of the member states. The ambience of simulated goodwill and regional bondage infused with indomitable desire were the driving force towards the adoption of working charter of this forum. The Article I of the Charter entails eight objectives of which the fifth one vouchsafes to provide active collaboration and mutual assistance in the economic, social, cultural, technical and scientific fields among the member states of the association. There are multiplicity of activities under the aegis of the SAARC forum to ensure economic prosperity, through trade and commerce, adequately supported by the performances in other areas like agriculture, telecommunications, health, transport, scientific and technical collaboration, art and culture as well as sports. While all the efforts are unquestionably laudable, one important area i.e., anthropological aspect of the population of the SAARC countries has conspicuously remained unnoticed.

The anthropological information of the population of the member states of SAARC provides fundamental inputs towards understanding their age-old bio-cultural relationship. The objectives of the SAARC are primarily oriented to strengthen the bondage of mutual co-operation among the concerned countries for the benefit of its population and the anthropological feedback at this juncture promises to act as catalist to achieve the target as set forth.

Being deeply concerned with the state of affairs as outlined above, the Anthropological Survey of India under its Ninth Plan programmes, commissioned a research project which sought to provide a compendium containing bio-cultural information on the populations of the SAARC countries. Since time immemorial, there had been migration of populations from one to other countries owing to various socio-economic, political and geo-environmental reasons. This has resulted in frequent exchange of thoughts, cultural elements, knowledge and in some instances free flow of genes, the biological materials. As a consequence strong ethno-historical bondage has been established among the population of the SAARC countries. Though there are sporadic records indicating close contact in various secondary sources as well as in repositories, but the need of systemic accounts is strongly felt. On the other hand there are evidences available in the folk traditions as well as in archaeological relics. All these information require our immediate attention to compile a comprehensive account in order to fortify the SAARC movement by way of providing further intellectual feedback.

From the ancient period, the population of Indian subcontinent was composed of many diverse racial elements and inhabited from the Old Stone Age onwards, despite its natural barriers like difficult mountain passes and the wide seas. Basham (1975) pointed out that these were probably the ancestors of one of India's three main races. The Proto-Australoid who resemble the Australian aborigines, are mainly found among the tribals of the wilder parts of the peninsula though such features could be traced everywhere in the subcontinent, especially among the people of low caste. These people are short in stature, dark-skinned, broad-nosed and large-mouthed. The next is the Palaeo-Mediterranean or loosely called Dravidian. These people perhaps came to South Asia from the west, not very long before the dawn of Indus Valley Civilisation, and they were the founders of Harrapan culture. They were graceful and slender, with well-chiselled features and aquiline nose. Such type is to be found among the upper caste speakers of Dravidian languages along with the other people of the subcontinent. In the second millennium B.C. the Aryans, speakers of an Indo-European language came. Perhaps these people came in two or more waves. The first group of people were round-headed (brachycephalic) popularly known as Alpine or Armenoid, and the second one were long-headed (dolichocephalic) or typical Caucasoid type. It is said that long before they entered India, these Aryans had intermixed with other peoples, hence, the Aryan culture became intermixed with indigenous culture which helped the formation of classical civilisation of India (Basham 1975). They overran the whole country and crossed over to Sri Lanka during the early centuries of pre-Christian era. They are also intermixed with the autochthonous population, thereby bringing about many changes in physical features. The Indo-Aryans were followed by the Irano-Scythians who brought and induced mesocephalic ethnic strain in the Indian population. The brachycephalic population of India is said to have originated through four different sources, the horders of Central Asia (Pamir), the Malayan, the Mongolian and the Irano-Scythian. The Mundas who appear to have migrated to India along the eastern coast have also contributed dolichocephalic element in Indian population (Sarkar 1953).

It is quite apparent that India reciprocated live contacts with many lands both far and near for mutual advantage and enriched the culture and civilisation of both the places. The religious philosophy, artistic motifs, economic plans, political knowledge had been exchanged between the people of these countries through traders, invaders, wondering monks, travellers etc. The course of the history of India and the neighbouring countries are very interesting as they have developed in both harmonious and in conflicting situations.

The long cultural heritage of the Indian subcontinent became enriched with devotional religion centering round the Lord Vishnu and Lord Shiva and the text composed in the form of *Bhagavad Gita*. Along with these, two great epics, the *Ramayana* and the *Mahabharata* developed. A good number of religious teachers took birth in this country while many philosophical schools emerged. With the development of communication facilities, the South Asian countries became closer through the spread of trade and these countries began to adapt many features of the religion and culture of India.

There are some close similarities discernible among the SAARC countries. India, Pakistan and Bangladesh have almost same political as well as cultural history and the latter two countries are the co-heirs of the historical, social and cultural legacy of India. Bhutan and Nepal are the two

Himalayan states in close proximity with the two giants of Asia viz., China and India. Both these nations have monarchial background. The two island countries Sri Lanka and Maldives had experience of either British rule or as a protectorate of the British empire.

The specific objective of the present exercise is to understand the biological and cultural relationship among the people of the SAARC countries, by way of retrieving and compiling information from available secondary sources. The information on biological aspect is restricted to morphological (anthropometric) and selected sero-genetic markers like ABO, Rh, Sickle-cell and G6PD besides prehistoric, proto-historic and archaeological data collected from published literature. An attempt has been made in 'Biological Perspectives' to review the information so generated and to discuss the situation in the context of ethno-history and population migration.

The study on the cultural aspect is limited upto the medieval period only. Pakistan and Bangladesh have not been dealt separately as these two were a part of India during the British rule. As the Indian subcontinent occupies a greater landmass of South Asia, the great Indus and Vedic civilisation developed here along with two major religious philosophy – Hinduism and Buddhism, we have made an attempt to understand the linkages of India with other countries of South Asia. This is not an exercise of reconstruction of historical facts. As mentioned earlier, only an attempt has been made here to retrieve information on the cultural linkages that the people of India once had with those of the other present SAARC countries. We intend to be familiar with the whole situation of the various SAARC countries separately as they existed during ancient and medieval periods. We do not claim to solve issues related to the origin and growth of civilisation of these countries. We only attempt to retrieve the facts available in the published secondary sources and set them down for drawing some trends on the basis of cultural traits similar to all those seven countries of South Asia.

We further attempt to examine the nature of sporadic influx of Indian traders and other immigrants to these lands resulting in diffusion of arts, crafts, customs and religions from India, including the use of Sanskrit and Pali as their sacred language. Prevalence of some traits of Hindu and Buddhist faiths, traces of mythology of Puranas and *Dharma Shastras*, and epics may shed some light in ascertaining the cultural linkage.

In order to accomplish the objectives, we have made an attempt to bring into relief the patterns of linkage as apparent in some aspects in 'Cultural Perspectives' like

- Mythologies and chronicles
- Occasional visits of the traders from one country to other through various routes with a view to extending new areas of economic transaction
- Spread of particular religion(s) which facilitated establishment of emotional bondage and also form(s)
- The pattern of diffusion of art and architecture among the populations of these countries during the ancient and medieval period of history.

available in the published secondary sources and set them down for drawing some trends on the basis of cultural traits similar to all those seven countries of South Asia.

We further attempt to examine the nature of sporadic influx of Indian traders and other immigrants to these lands resulting in diffusion of arts, crafts, customs and religions from India, including the use of Sanskrit and Pali as their sacred language. Prevalence of some traits of Hindu and Buddhist faiths, traces of mythology of Puranas and *Dharma Shastras*, and epics may shed some light in ascertaining the cultural linkage.

In order to accomplish the objectives, we have made an attempt to bring into relief the patterns of linkage as apparent in some aspects in 'Cultural Perspectives' like

- Mythologies and chronicles
- Occasional visits of the traders from one country to other through various routes with a view to extending new areas of economic transaction
- Spread of particular religion(s) which facilitated establishment of emotional bondage and also form(s)
- The pattern of diffusion of art and architecture among the populations of these countries during the ancient and medieval period of history.

Himalayan states in close proximity with the two giants of Asia viz., China and India. Both these nations have monarchial background. The two island countries Sri Lanka and Maldives had experience of either British rule or as a protectorate of the British empire.

The specific objective of the present exercise is to understand the biological and cultural relationship among the people of the SAARC countries, by way of retrieving and compiling information from available secondary sources. The information on biological aspect is restricted to morphological (anthropometric) and selected sero-genetic markers like ABO, Rh, Sickle-cell and G6PD besides prehistoric, proto-historic and archaeological data collected from published literature. An attempt has been made in 'Biological Perspectives' to review the information so generated and to discuss the situation in the context of ethno-history and population migration.

The study on the cultural aspect is limited upto the medieval period only. Pakistan and Bangladesh have not been dealt separately as these two were a part of India during the British rule. As the Indian subcontinent occupies a greater landmass of South Asia, the great Indus and Vedic civilisation developed here along with two major religious philosophy – Hinduism and Buddhism, we have made an attempt to understand the linkages of India with other countries of South Asia. This is not an exercise of reconstruction of historical facts. As mentioned earlier, only an attempt has been made here to retrieve information on the cultural linkages that the people of India once had with those of the other present SAARC countries. We intend to be familiar with the whole situation of the various SAARC countries separately as they existed during ancient and medieval periods. We do not claim to solve issues related to the origin and growth of civilisation of these countries. We only attempt to retrieve the facts population, thereby bringing about many changes in physical features. The Indo-Aryans were followed by the Irano-Scythians who brought and induced mesocephalic ethnic strain in the Indian population. The brachycephalic population of India is said to have originated through four different sources, the horders of Central Asia (Pamir), the Malayan, the Mongolian and the Irano-Scythian. The Mundas who appear to have migrated to India along the eastern coast have also contributed dolichocephalic element in Indian population (Sarkar 1953).

It is quite apparent that India reciprocated live contacts with many lands both far and near for mutual advantage and enriched the culture and civilisation of both the places. The religious philosophy, artistic motifs, economic plans, political knowledge had been exchanged between the people of these countries through traders, invaders, wondering monks, travellers etc. The course of the history of India and the neighbouring countries are very interesting as they have developed in both harmonious and in conflicting situations.

The long cultural heritage of the Indian subcontinent became enriched with devotional religion centering round the Lord Vishnu and Lord Shiva and the text composed in the form of *Bhagavad Gita*. Along with these, two great epics, the *Ramayana* and the *Mahabharata* developed. A good number of religious teachers took birth in this country while many philosophical schools emerged. With the development of communication facilities, the South Asian countries became closer through the spread of trade and these countries began to adapt many features of the religion and culture of India.

There are some close similarities discernible among the SAARC countries. India, Pakistan and Bangladesh have almost same political as well as cultural history and the latter two countries are the co-heirs of the historical, social and cultural legacy of India. Bhutan and Nepal are the two information require our immediate attention to compile a comprehensive account in order to fortify the SAARC movement by way of providing further intellectual feedback.

From the ancient period, the population of Indian subcontinent was composed of many diverse racial elements and inhabited from the Old Stone Age onwards, despite its natural barriers like difficult mountain passes and the wide seas. Basham (1975) pointed out that these were probably the ancestors of one of India's three main races. The Proto-Australoid who resemble the Australian aborigines, are mainly found among the tribals of the wilder parts of the peninsula though such features could be traced everywhere in the subcontinent, especially among the people of low caste. These people are short in stature, dark-skinned, broad-nosed and large-mouthed. The next is the Palaeo-Mediterranean or loosely called Dravidian. These people perhaps came to South Asia from the west, not very long before the dawn of Indus Valley Civilisation, and they were the founders of Harrapan culture. They were graceful and slender, with well-chiselled features and aquiline nose. Such type is to be found among the upper caste speakers of Dravidian languages along with the other people of the subcontinent. In the second millennium B.C. the Aryans, speakers of an Indo-European language came. Perhaps these people came in two or more waves. The first group of people were round-headed (brachycephalic) popularly known as Alpine or Armenoid, and the second one were long-headed (dolichocephalic) or typical Caucasoid type. It is said that long before they entered India, these Aryans had intermixed with other peoples, hence, the Aryan culture became intermixed with indigenous culture which helped the formation of classical civilisation of India (Basham 1975). They overran the whole country and crossed over to Sri Lanka during the early centuries of pre-Christian era. They are also intermixed with the autochthonous the association. There are multiplicity of activities under the aegis of the SAARC forum to ensure economic prosperity, through trade and commerce, adequately supported by the performances in other areas, like agriculture, telecommunications, health, transport, scientific and technical collaboration, art and culture as well as sports. While all the efforts are unquestionably laudable, one important area i.e., anthropological aspect of the population of the SAARC countries has conspicuously remained unnoticed.

The anthropological information of the population of the member states of SAARC provides fundamental inputs towards understanding their age-old bio-cultural relationship. The objectives of the SAARC are primarily oriented to strengthen the bondage of mutual co-operation among the concerned countries for the benefit of its population and the anthropological feedback at this juncture promises to act as catalist to achieve the target as set forth.

Being deeply concerned with the state of affairs as outlined above, the Anthropological Survey of India under its Ninth Plan programmes, commissioned a research project which sought to provide a compendium containing bio-cultural information on the populations of the SAARC countries. Since time immemorial, there had been migration of populations from one to other countries owing to various socio-economic, political and geo-environmental reasons. This has resulted in frequent exchange of thoughts, cultural elements, knowledge and in some instances free flow of genes, the biological materials. As a consequence strong ethno-historical bondage has been established among the population of the SAARC countries. Though there are sporadic records indicating close contact in various secondary sources as well as in repositories, but the need of systemic accounts is strongly felt. On the other hand there are evidences available in the folk traditions as well as in archaeological relics. All these

Introduction

G.C. Ghosh and J.K. Sarkar

South Asia, consisting of India, Pakistan, Bangladesh, Sri Lanka, Maldives, Bhutan and Nepal is a large landmass containing one fifth of the total global population. This region is enormously rich in terms of biotic and abiotic resources. It has a huge forest coverage and endless source of minerals coupled with viable human resource endowment. In spite of all the basic components and inherent natural wealth, progress and development of this region suffer a glaring set back. This is partly because of the colonial legacy of subjugation under which the area had to pass through. The urge for consorted effort for the benefit of the economically weak and the underdeveloped human souls mooted the concept towards formation of a common forum, 'South Asian Association for Regional Cooperation' (SAARC) in August 1980. This idea received intellectual nourishment on account of common ethnic, social, cultural and historical background of the member states. The ambience of simulated goodwill and regional bondage infused with indomitable desire were the driving force towards the adoption of working charter of this forum. The Article I of the Charter entails eight objectives of which the fifth one vouchsafes to provide active collaboration and mutual assistance in the economic, social, cultural, technical and scientific fields among the member states of

Contents

Foreword   v
Preface   vii
Introduction
   G.C. Ghosh and J.K. Sarkar   1

Part-I
Biological Perspectives

1. Biological Relationship of the Populations of Sri Lanka, Maldives and Pakistan with Those of India
   Chumki Piplai   9

2. Biological Affinities of the Populations of Nepal, Bhutan and Bangladesh with Those of India
   J.M. Sarkar   39

Part-II
Cultural Perspectives

3. Cultural Linkages Among the People of India, Sri Lanka, Nepal, Bhutan and Maldives
   Jyotirmoy Chakraborty and Rabiranjan Biswas   55

4. Epilogue
   J.K. Sarkar and G.C. Ghosh   126
   References   143
   About the Contributors   159

Preface

South Asian Association for Regional Cooperation (SAARC) was formed in August 1980. This necessitated dissemination of knowledge all over the globe in respect of the life and culture of the people of its member nations in order to build up a mass-based stable relation so that the common people could appreciate each others' cultural heritage, removing many misconceptions. There is no dearth of literature, specially on the contemporary economic and political situations of the SAARC countries. However, unfortunately there hardly exists any anthropological literature, which comprehensively put forth the biological affinities and cultural relations of the people of these nations since early period of history and prehistory.

The present book, *Populations of the SAARC Countries: Biocultural Perspectives*, is an attempt to bring together all such fragmented information in various forms, which are available in scattered manner in published materials in different languages. An anthropological analysis and interpretation of such information has reaffirmed the presence of cultural linkages and biological affiliation even in the distant past.

A number of issues delineated in this work are expected to inspire scholars and academicians in searching many more unknown realms of biological and cultural linkages of the populations of the SAARC nations. The editors are thankful to Sterling Publishers Private Limited who has shown interest in bringing out this publication.

Editors

Part-I
Biological Perspectives

Biological Relationship of the Populations of Sri Lanka, Maldives and Pakistan with Those of India

Chumki Piplai

Introduction

People are migrating since the prehistoric time. During their movement, people mixed with different groups in different times and consequently got detached from the mainstream. Their contribution to genetic material and cultural heritage are spread over the wide range, throughout their migration track. South Asia is a core area for the prehistoric, historic and even for modern migration. Evidences from history and archaeology suggest people's movement in this particular area, which could be confirmed by their genetic, morphological, cultural and linguistic variation and affinities.

Migration of people from India to its neighbouring countries, particularly in the SAARC countries, is a prehistoric phenomenon, which still continues. Consequences of such movements have been discussed in the following pages through examination of the extent of biological affinities, which are apparent among the population of Sri Lanka, Maldives and Pakistan.

Sri Lanka

Sri Lanka is a pear-shaped island situated in the Indian Ocean having a total area of 65,610 sq. km. The island is 430 km. long and 230 km. across its widest point. The total population of Sri Lanka is estimated about 14,346,750 (1981 census). The south-east tip of India is only thirty-five kilometres away from the shoreline of Sri Lanka. It is on the ocean ridge between East Africa and South Asia, providing a natural stepping for the traders. Early Greeks and Europeans knew the island which was visited by Marco Polo in 1293 A.D. The Portugese were the first Europeans to land on this island in 1505 A.D. Subsequently it was occupied by the Dutch. At the end of the eighteenth century the Dutch were challenged by the British who captured the fort of Colombo and it came under the rule of British East India Company in 1802.

History of Migration

Sinhalese trace their origin to pre-Buddhist invaders from northern India. Their most ancient chronicle, *Mahavamsa*, depicts the transplantation of Indian organisation. Movement of Indians to Sri Lanka began during the sixth century B.C. (now settled in northern jungles). The passage of centuries saw the sources of Indian influence and the migrants to Sri Lanka shifted from north India to Deccan. After the tenth century A.D. south Indian princes were indeed established as rulers in the northern part of the island, while to the east and south the Sinhalese maintained their kingdoms, the last of which, the Kandyan, capitulated to the British in 1815.

According to the popular myth, the Sinhalese are direct descendants of Aryan speaking people who founded their ancient civilisation. This view is more nationalistic than historic. According to Denham (1912):

The Sinhalese are a composite people not only of pre-christian era invaders, but of migrating tribal groups, remnants of Tamil invasions, and others. Even among the Kandyans, occupying the interior of the island, it is reasonable to believe that intermittent tribal infusions were not lacking.

Evidences favouring this view are given in various context. For the Kandyan area, Denham marked some relevant observation, and the Sinhalese epics – *Mahavasmsha* and *Dipavamsha*, indicate the introduction of Indian mercenaries and captives. Regarding the late movement of south Indians and others into the low country, there were cultural evidences of south Indian connection among several low country Sinhalese castes. Edmund Reimere (cited from Maloney 1980) has found documentary corroboration of large-scale movements of mercenaries into Ceylon from Coromondal and Malabar coasts in the mid fifteenth century. During the second century A.D. King Karikala of Cholas, from Kaveri delta, invaded Sri Lanka and took away 12,000 prisoners of war to construct his irrigation works. Further tradition was that the Sinhala King Gajabahu later took 12,000 (or 24,000) Chola prisoners to Sri Lanka in retaliation (Pillai 1963).

In the first five centuries after the north Indian migration, the major factors influencing Sri Lanka's ancient history had emerged. Apart from the establishment of the Sinhalese as a group with a common culture, which included the impact of Buddha, and the development of an agriculture based economy, partly with irrigation facilities, a series of efforts were made to draw a political unit. Besides Indian connection, Portuguese, Dutch, Arab and British also contributed much in the biological and cultural sphere.

Population

The Veddas are considered to be the autochthonous group in Sri Lanka. According to Tresidder (1960) the inhabitants of Sri Lanka are:

Sri Lankan people and their combination

Population	Combination
1 Veddas	Descendants of aboriginal tribes (before coming of Indian primitive settlers)
2 Low country Sinhalese	Decendants of local Veddas and Malabaries
3 Kandyan Sinhalese	Descendants of local people and north Indian people
4 Sri Lankan Tamils	Many came from Malaya or other South East Asian countries
5 Sri Lankan Moors (Muslims)	Descendants of Arabian merchants and local women
6 Indian Tamils	South Indian origin
7 Indian Moors	Immigrants from Borah sect from Bombay and South India
8 Burgher	Dutch European and Sinhalese (Muslims)
9 Malayans	Descendants of Sinhalese and Tamils
10 Kaffirs	Originally imported as slaves or soldiers by the Sinhalese
11 Other groups	Migrants from Afganistan, Baluchistan, Bombay, Goa and South India.

Affinities From Prehistoric and Archaeological Evidences

Sri Lanka enters the broad arena of old world human paleontology (Map-1) with a fossil record dating to 26,500 B.C., a period relatively contemporary with anatomically modern Homo sapiens fossil recovered elsewhere (Kennedy and Deraniyagala 1989). During the last one million years when humans are known to have existed in various parts of India (Mishra 1995), Sri Lanka was connected to Indian subcontinent at different phases of time. The rise and fall of

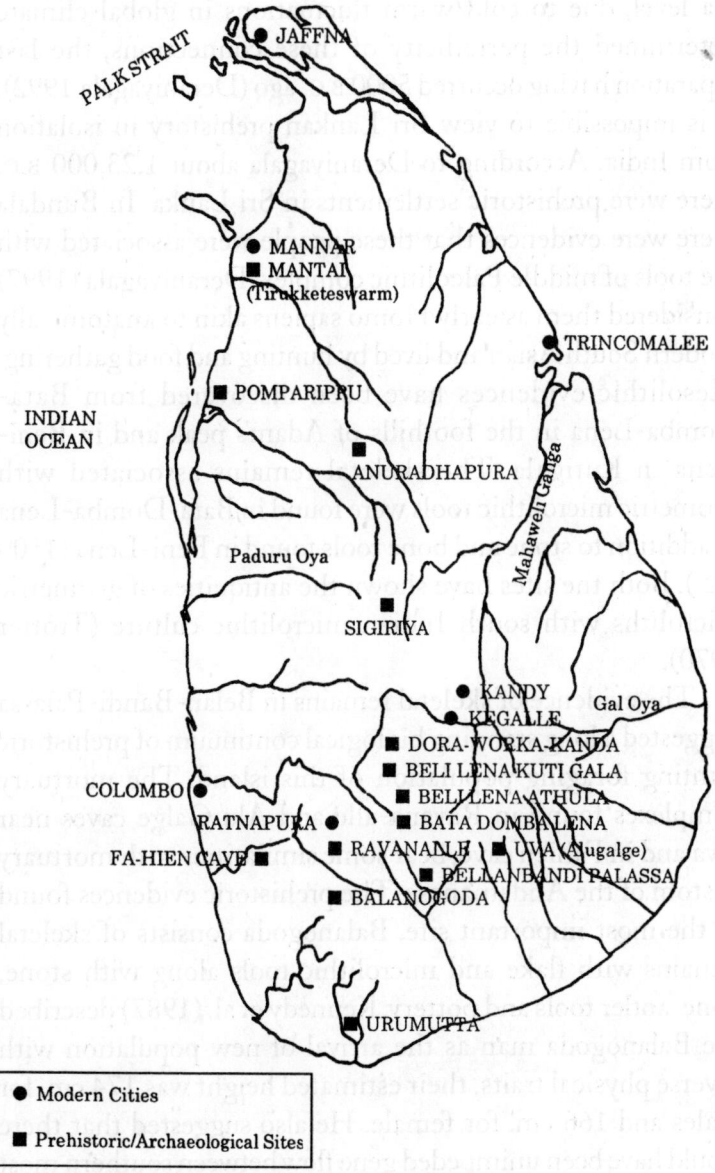

Map-1: Distribution of Prehistoric and Archaeological Sites in Sri Lanka

sea level, due to cold/warm fluctuations in global climate determined the periodicity of these connections, the last separation having occurred 5000 B.C. ago (Deraniyagala 1992). It is impossible to view Sri Lankan prehistory in isolation from India. According to Deraniyagala about 1,23,000 B.C. there were prehistoric settlements in Sri Lanka. In Bundala there were evidences that these people were associated with the tools of middle Paleolithic complex. Deraniyagala (1997) considered them as early Homo sapiens akin to anatomically modern South Asian and lived by hunting and food gathering. Mesolithic evidences have been discovered from Bata-Domba-Lena in the foothills of Adam's peak and in Beni-Lena in Kutigala. The skeletal remains associated with geometric microlithic tools were found in Bata-Domba-Lena in addition to stone and bone tools found in Beni-Lena (1500 B.C.). Both the sites have shown the antiquities of geometric microliths with south Indian microlithic culture (Trotter 1970).

The evidence of skeletal remains in Belan-Bandi-Palassa suggested a long standing biological continuum of prehistoric hunting foraging population of this island. The mortuary complexes found in Ravana-alle and Alu Galge caves near Uva and in Fahien cave, bear some similarities with mortuary custom of the Andamanese. The prehistoric evidences found in the most important site, Balanogoda consists of skeletal remains with flake and microlithic tools along with stone, bone, antler tools and pottery. Kennedy et al. (1987) described the Balanogoda man as the arrival of new population with diverse physical traits, their estimated height was 174 cm. for males and 166 cm. for female. He also suggested that there would have been unimpeded gene flow between southern most India and Sri Lanka in both directions, from the Paleolithic period onward. According to him, their lifestyles could not have been too different from the Veddas of Sri Lanka, the

Kadars, the Malapantrams, the Chenchus and the Andaman Islanders of India. They would have been moving from place to place on an annual cycle for food. Their diet was well balanced as attested by the robusticity of the skeletal remains.

The discovery of a few pieces of copper working-slag from the Mesolithic contexts at Matota signifying the first identification of Chalcolithic horizon of Sri Lanka, are contemporary to the Chalcolithic period of the peninsular India. It is now known that the major source of copper ore lying south of Madhya Pradesh was located at Seruvila in eastern Sri Lanka (Seneviratne 1984). This was known to the Chalcolithic people of India and the Sri Lankans also exploited this source. It may be assured that Mantai in Sri Lanka could well have been a port for shipping copper to India.

Evidences unearthed from Dora-Worka-Kanda were black and red ware pottery, fertiliser and polished axe resembling to south Indian Neolithic culture (Wijayapala 1992).

The proto-historic early Iron Age was established as early as 1200 B.C. in south India. The earliest manifestation of this was in Anuradhapura and Sigiriya which was dated as c 1000 – 800 B.C. (Deraniyagala 1992). The megalithic early Iron Age mortuary complex of Sri Lanka (Seneviratne 1984) is akin to that of peninsular India and the only site excavated till date is Ibbankatutwa. Here megalithic cemetery is absent but it is associated with megalithic mortuary complex of the pastoral group, those occupied in Anuradhapura (Leshink 1974). The megalithic mortuary trait is discrete facet of the proto-historic early Iron Age culture complex of India, distributed from the Gangetic valley down to Sri Lanka with regional variation.

The biological anthropology of early Iron Age man of Sri Lanka is distinct from Balanogoda man, although evidences from the only megalithic site of Pomparippu suggests a certain degree of miscegenation. The archaeological evidences from Pomparippu in north-west Sri Lanka had considerable influence of south Indian megalithic culture over the region at least by the third century B.C. Style of urn burials, the pottery and other objects found in Pomparippu are similar to the objects found in Adittanalur site across the Gulf of Mannar in India. While cultural influence does not necessarily imply migration or inter-marriage, it is important to remember that at that time the ethnic identities of these groups of people were not developed strongly enough to keep them distinct (De Silva 1987).

As noticed by Deraniyagala (1997), abundant supplies of water, iron-technology to subjugate the dense equatorial rainforest, heavy soils, pearl banks in the north-west Islands, copper sources at Seruvila and the land's location as an entrepot for long distance trade between South-East Asia and West Asia, attracted the people to Sri Lanka. Thereafter Sri Lanka's attraction for settlers from distant place other than the south India occurred rapidly. This wave was considered as the so-called second urbanisation of the Indo-Gangetic people (Allchin 1995).

The onset of urbanisation in Sri Lanka by 500 B.C. was accelerated in the early historic period, at the time of Ashoka in the 300 B.C. Buddhism probably manifested early in Sri Lanka either through rapid stimulus diffusion, or convergent evolution as well as long distance trade, or combination of both. Buddhism was introduced in Sri Lanka from the Ashoka epoch which had some link with the archaeological site of Anuradhapura that was peopled from 200 B.C. The cultural connection with south India are clearly evident here. The sculpture found are related to those of Kushan style (seated figure), rather than to those of Amaravati (Satbahan empire). The remarkable paintings from Sigiriya have affinities with Amaravati and Pallava style. Physical features of the figures are Sinhalese but owes much to India (Cottrell 1960). These findings suggest transaction of culture and art among the people of Sri Lanka and south India.

Physical features of the Sri Lankan Buddhists are akin to the features of the Bengalis. Interestingly even after about three thousand years of the invasion of Vijaya and his disciple, their features are similar to north Indians. A large number of Bengalis took to Buddhism and settled in Sri Lanka. This migration ceased after the reign of the Sen dynasty. Hence the Bengalis migrated to Sri Lanka before seven or eight generations ago are not uncommon there. Besides, the merchants' sail for Sri Lanka has been described in Mongol Kabya, Satyapirer Panchali or Sonir Panchali (Sen 1993). Jagadiswarm (1933) is of the opinion that:

> The Sinhalese who form a vast majority of the Ceylonese are descendants of the Vijaya, the Bengali prince, and hence the language, specially the Singhalese has close affinity with the Bengali. Both Singhalese and the Bengali belong to the same stock of north Indian Aryan and so have many things in common.

Biological Affinities with the Indians

The Veddas of Sri Lanka are classified as Proto-Australoid in terms of morphological characters. All the tribes of central and southern India are described as Proto-Australoid for their close affinities with the Australian tribes in "stature, shape of the head, protrusion of facial parts, broad flat nose, fleshy everted lips and skin colour" (Guha 1944). More recent studies (Kirk 1976, Simmon 1976, Roy Choudhury 1983) refute the affinity of the tribes of southern India and Sri Lanka with the Australian aborigines (Bhalla 1989).

S.W. Kulatilake compared the Veddas, the north Indians including the population of Punjab, West Bengal and North-

West Province and Arabians using 42 craniometric variables and found that the clusters of the north Indians and the Veddas are closer as they have strikingly similar cranial shape.

Considering mythological, historical and linguistic records of Sri Lanka, Kshatriya (1995) studied the degree of gene diversity and genetic admixture among the populations of Sri Lanka and India. In this study, the genetic distance analysis was conducted using 43 alleles controlled by 13 co-dominant loci in 8 populations and 40 alleles controlled by 13 co-dominant loci in 11 populations. The 13 polymorphic loci are ABO, MN, Rh, P, Hb, Hp, Tf, AcP, AK, ESD, PGD, PGM and G6PD. His analyses depict that present day Sinhalese and Tamils of Sri Lanka are closer to Indian Tamils, and south Indian Muslims. They are furthest from the Veddas and quite distant from the Gujaratis and Punjabis of north-west India and the Bengalis of east India.

The Sinhalese, Sri Lankan Tamils, Indian Tamils and south Indian Muslims form one cluster, whereas the Gujaratis, Punjabis, and west Indian Muslims form another cluster. These two clusters are distinct and do not show much affinities with the Bengalis and the Veddas. The dendrograms reveal close similarities between the Sinhalese and the Sri Lankan Tamils, Sinhalese and Indian Tamils and between Sri Lankan Tamils and Indian Tamils.

From the estimated values of genetic admixture of the two hybrid groups (Sinhalese and Tamils), it has been observed that the Sinhalese have a predominantly Tamil (India) contribution followed by the Bengalis and the Veddas. The fusion of the Veddas and the Sinhalese is recorded in the ancient chronicles of Sri Lanka. Among the Sri Lankan Tamils the contribution of the Sinhalese is 55.20 per cent, of the Bengalis 28.17 per cent and of the Indian Tamils 16.63 per cent. The original inhabitants of Sri Lanka were the Veddas who had little admixture with the Sinhalese, but none with the Tamils. The Veddas are distinct because they were confined to inhospitable dry zones and were hardly influenced by the neighbouring inhabitants, whereas the Sinhalese and the Sri Lankan Tamils are genetically admixed populations. Kshatriya's view on this study is that "the Sinhalese of Sri Lanka are genetically more similar to the Tamils of Sri Lanka and India, who were always in close proximity with each other historically, linguistically, geographically and culturally".

Kirk (1976) in his study in the area of Anuradhapura and Kandy found that the ancient chronicles relate the origin of the Sinhalese people of Sri Lanka to the arrival of Prince Vijaya from an area in north-east or north-west India and his subsequent affiliation with people from south India. Genetic distance analysis however, despite the limitation imposed by the data, show that modern Sinhalese populations are closer to the Tamils and Keralites of south India and the upper caste of Bengal than they are to Gujaratis or Punjabis.

Saha (1988) recorded another view in his study from the hospital sample in Singapore using serum protein, haemoglobin and red cell enzyme from the Sinhalese, Tamils, and Muslims of Sri Lanka. The allelic frequencies of all the polymorphic systems were similar in these populations without any significant differences.

The most reasonable interpretation appears to have been suggested by Kirk et al. (1962) taking into account the location of one of their Sinhalese samples, that some Sinhalese intermixed with the Tamils have attained an intermediate genetic composition. Hence the ancestral frequency of the Sinhalese should be considered from an opposite direction from the Tamils. The only pointer so far to the frequency characteristics of the people further north in India lies in MNS linkage group, and those are barely sufficient to set up hypothesis of genetic affinity of the present day Sinhalese population.

From this study it was concluded that differences existed between the gene frequencies of the Sinhalese and the Tamils. But tradition and culture suggested similarity between the Sinhalese and contiguous northern populations of today. Roy Choudhury (1984) showed that the south Indians were found to have close affinities with the Sinhalese as they settled in northern Sri Lanka for a long period. But historical evidence of north Indian migration was proved by existence of common traits like HbE and hairy pinnae in both the populations.

Papiha et al. (1996) studied 27 polymorphic and 3 monomorphic loci among the five main populations of Sri Lanka collected from Colombo. Several genetic markers including subtype variations of Hp, Tf, PI, GC, ORM and PGM1 were analysed for the first time and helped to clarify the range of genetic variation of Sri Lankan populations. Many genetic systems (Rh, JK, ACP, ESD, Hp, C_3, Tf, and GC) showed a high level of variation among them. The authors expressed that the present day gene pool of the populations of Sri Lanka must be highly influenced by admixture. Significant heterogeneity was found in the Rh, Kidd, ACP, ESD, C_3, GC, Hp and Tf system, and the test of heterogeneity of different alleles clearly revealed higher levels of diversity among the populations of Sri Lanka. These datas are quite comparable with other studies carried out where the samples were collected within Sri Lanka (Wickremasinghe et al. 1963, Kirk et al. 1962, Roberts, Creen et al. 1972, Roberts, Papiha et al. 1972). The ESC allele has been suggested as a European marker. But its presence in the Sinhalese indicates either admixture or an origin in northern India. Low value of ESD-5 in the Tamils can be attributed to their admixture with the Sinhalese. Thus little distance was observed between the oldest populations on the island, the Sinhalese and the Tamils (0.0142)

The Veddas of Sri Lanka, with a high frequency of B and a very low of A gene, differ greatly not only from the Sinhalese and the Tamil neighbours but also from other Indian communities including the Veddoid people of Tamil Nadu and Kerala. But they have a resemblance to the Kotas and the Nayadis who have practically no A gene and the Mullu Kurumbas who have very little. Mourant et al. (1976) is of the opinion that present Vedda communities of Sri Lanka have acquired genes of all kinds from the Tamils and Sinhalese and found low or absence of A gene or comparatively low M gene, high CDe and low CDE. In MNS system the similar situation was observed among the Chenchus, Pallars, Malapantarams, Malavedans and Mala Kuruvans of south India. High CDE and low CDE are also found in the Malapantarams, Pallars, Paniyans and the Kotas and to a lesser degree among the Chenchus.

Among the Asiatic populations Lu^a is very low. But the Veddas are almost the only population in South Asian region who possess Lu^a. They also possess high Fy^a, P_1 and K. The Chenchus of south India show similar frequency to the Veddas. HbE is exceptionally common in the Veddas and also among the Sinhalese. But it is not so in case of other south Indian tribes. The absence of HbS is remarkable among the Veddas. The occasional occurrence of thalassemia in the Veddas might show the relationship either to India or South-East Asian populations.

Mourant et al. (1976) express their views as:

> It is impossible to prove that they were not derived from relatively recent intermarriage with the Sinhalese and Tamils, but it would not be surprising if as a result of pressure from the repeated invasions which India has received from the north, members of varied populations which now inhabit the southern tip of India had before, and perhaps long before, the coming of the ancestors of the present Sinhalese, gradually infiltered into Ceylon.

Mourant et al. (1976) also found that the Veddas possess A_2, cde, and MS from Indian source. Again the Padhu or Bathgamuwa of eastern Sri Lanka who are likely to be the Veddoids of southern India posses HbS, CDE or Rz and have a high frequency of A_1 (Studied by Wickremasinghe et al. 1963; only from 19 samples). Mourant et al. (1976) considered them as the Veddoid rather than the Veddas. They also assumed that, if their ancestors did indeed come from India, they might have arrived even before the Malay ancestors of the Veddas. Mourant also suggested for the further research on both anthropology and archaeology as well as the history of the early inhabitants of Sri Lanka and their present descendants in order to clear the situation.

From the above discussions it is apparent that the populations of Sri Lanka particularly the Sinhalese, possess some biological traits which are similar to those of the north and south Indians (Table 1). The Sinhalese who speak Aryan language descent from central India (Roberts et al. 1972). Modern Sinhalese are closer to the Tamils and the Keralites of south India and upper caste of Bengal (Kirk 1962). Papiha et al. (1996) and Khatriya (1995) are of the views that the Sinhalese may be either admixture or have an origin in north Indian populations and at the same time south Indian Tamils. But it is to be kept in mind that several intruders are mixed with the aboriginal inhabitants of this region and metamorphosis occurred in different time and phases. The isolated people may bear their primitive characters, but exposure to different genetic material introduced a higher level of diversity.

Table 1 : Biological Affinities between Sri Lankans and Indian Population

Population	Affinity	Trait
Vedda of Sri Lanka	Resembles with central and south Indian tribes like Kadars, Malapantrams, Chenchus and others. (Simmon 1976; Roy Choudhury 1984) Mixture of Australoid, African and Mediterranean (DeSilva 1981) Resembles with the Kotas, Nayadis, Mulla-Kurumbas, Mala Kuruvans, Pallars, Mala Pantrams and the Mala Vedans (Bhalla 1989)	Physical features ABO, MNS
	Acquired many genes from the Tamils and Sinhalese (Mourant et al. 1976)	
Sinhalese and Tamils of Sri Lanka	Close to north Indian (Punjab, West Bengal) population (Kulatilake 1996)	ABO, Rh, MS, Lu, Fy, K (Chenchu) HbS', HbE (Sinhalese)
	Closer to the Indian Tamils and Indian Muslims	Craniometry
		Genetic distance analysis using 43 alleles controlled by 13 loci (ABO, MN, Rh,P, Hb, Hp, Tf, ACP, AK, ESD, PGD, PGM, G6PD)
	Furthest from the Veddas, quite distant from the	Genetic distance analysis using 40

Population	Affinity	Trait
	Gujaratis, Punjabis and Bengalis	alleles controlled by 13 co-dominant loci
	Sinhalese have predominantly Tamil contribution followed by the Bengalis and Veddas (Kshatriya et al. 1995)	Estimated value of genetic admixture of two hybrid groups
Sinhalese	Sinhalese are similar to north-east Indian (Bengali) and some of them have Tamil admixture (Kirk et al. 1962)	ABO, MNS
Sinhalese, Tamil and Muslim of Sri Lanka	Highly influenced by admixture (Papiha et al. 1996)	Rh, JK, PGM, ACP, ESD, Hp, C3, TF, GC
-Do-	Not close to east Indian (Saha et al. 1988)	13 polymorphic characters

Maldives

The republic of Maldives is about 400 miles to the south-west of Sri Lanka. It consists of 12,000 low lying coral islands grouped into 26 atoll of which only 210 are inhabited. Anand (1997) observed that the islands are populated by different groups those are descendants of the Veddas, Sinhalese, Dravidians from Sri Lanka and India, Arabians and the Negros. Maldives has been independent except for a brief period of Portuguese rule in the sixteenth century. It was under British protection from 1887 to 1965 and became a republic in 1968.

History of Migration

Archaeological finds reveal that the islands were inhabited as early as 1500 B.C. However it is belived that the first settlers in the islands were Aryan immigrants who came around 500 B.C. Today Maldivian are a mixed race (Grover 1997).

The origin of Maldivian is yet to be fully known. Roy (1912) had observed that the dialects of the aboriginal people of Maldives are similar to the Mundari group and Semang of Malaya. According to Maloney there were Dravidian people from south India as early as the fourth century B.C. Tamils and Keralites occupied Maldives and subsequently were absorbed into Divehi population who had migrated from south India and Sri Lanka. The Aryans from India and Sri Lanka came latter to dominate the islands. Buddhism was widely practised until 1153 when the ruling dynasty embraced Islam and ordered the people to do likewise. Today nearly cent per cent of Maldivians belong to Sunni faith of Islam.

According to Coelho (1997), the Maldivian claim to belong to the Aryan race. In fact, one of the titles of the Sultans has traditionally been a great ruler of the universe, a kshatriya of pure race. However there is evidence of distinct and different ethnic origins among the people such as Sinhalese, Dravidians and Arabic (or Sematic).

Bowels (1977) described the Maldives and Lakshwadeep islanders as mixed populations between Malayali inhabitants and Arab intruders. The genetic stability of the population is far more distinctive which classifies them with their Malabar coast neighbours.

According to H.C.P. Bell (1940) earliest migrants to the islands were the Gujaratis followed by Divehi speaking group from Sri Lanka, indigenous Dravidian speakers from Sri Lanka, Malayalis, Mappilas from Kerala, Tamils from south India (East Coast), traders from south-east India and Bengal (Table 2). The Gujaratis arrived in the Maldives during the Indus Valley Civilisation through Gujarat port and Bharukachha. Most of the people were traders and they came from Malabar coast, Kerala, Chittagong (now in Bangladesh),

Orissa and Uttar Pradesh. North Indian land-owning caste (Thakur), sailor and boatman (Takkra) and the Bohra Muslims of Gujarat also migrated there. There is an element of Divehi (Sri Lankan) that represents a separate and early migration from the coast of north-west India to Maldives. Malabari seafarers having found and settled in Lakshadweep Islands, would have gone on to settle in Maldives, possibly after their earlier discovery by the Gujarati seafarers. There is substantial evidence that the Maldives was traditionally ruled by the queens, which is akin to the origin of the matrilineal inheritance of the people of Maliku (Minicoy). It is evident from Kautilya's *Arthashastra* that sea routes for Indo-Sri Lankan trades at the time of Maurya empire, were well-known. The Gujaratis or other merchants from western India probably knew of Maldives during the second century B.C. and before Tamils began wide ranging seafaring. During third or second century B.C. Tamil-Malayalis had the technical capacity to settle and populated the Maldives.

Table 2 : Ethnic Migration from India to Maldives

Inhabitant of Maldives	Migrant from
Gujarati	Gujarat
Malayali	Kerala
Mapilla	-do-
Tamil	East Coast of Tamil Nadu
Traders	South-eastern India, Malabar, Orissa, Kerala, Uttar Pradesh, Chitagang (Presently in Bangladesh)
Thakur	Uttar Pradesh
Takkra (sailor and boatman)	Gujarat
Bohra Muslim	-do-
Divehi Speaker	Sri Lanka
Dravidian Speaker	-do-

Nag (1997) described that:

> The history of the island is largely unrecorded and somewhat vague. The people originally migrated from India. Nobody knows when, but it was a long time ago. At first they were Buddhist, then about 500 years ago the Arabs came and converted them to Islam. In the early nineteenth century they came under the Portuguese. In 1887 they became British protectories.

Grover (1997) opined that, "Malabari pirates from the nearby south Indian coast succeeded in 1752 in seizing the Maldivian throne in the Capital of Male and in 1887 under British protectories". He also described them as a Divehi speaking group, akin to Elu or old Sinhalese. Their economy depends on fish and coconut and other food products like millets and fruits. The principal industry is fishing besides copra production, coir yarn and merchant shipping.

Coelho (1997) found them as engaged in lacquer work, weaving of fine mats, lace making and carving wooden vessels. It is interesting to note that short, fine chisel like tools are used in tracing and carving the design on wood work. Maldives has no evidence of prehistoric antiquities, as because it is an atoll.

Genetic Affinities

Madaan (1977) considered the Maldivians as a mixed people belonging to Dravidian and Sinhalese stock.

In physical appearance and language, there is a marked affinity between the Maldivians and the Sri Lankans (Nuri 1997). It is said that the inhabitants are descendants of the Veddas, Sinhalese, Dravidians from Sri Lanka and India and the Arabs (Anand 1997). Kalra (1947) opined that the Maldivians were Singhalese in origin with higher O (58.3 per cent) and lower A (17.5 per cent) blood group. He also observed a considerable inbreeding for a few centuries, which caused a small population group of less than two thousand individuals. It may be mentioned here that the higher frequency of O blood groups is also observed among the inhabitants of Lakshadweep (Bhattacharya and Biswas 1978).

Systematic bio-anthropological studies are yet to be undertaken among the Maldivians. Due to lack of information it is not possible here to discuss their biological relationship with the Indians. This calls for attention to undertake studies on the morphogenetic aspect of the Maldivians in the context of ethnological and migratory history of the populations of India and Maldives.

Pakistan

Pakistan is bounded in the north-west by Afganistan, north by China, east by India and south by Arabian sea. Population as per 1981 census (excluding Azad Kashmir, Baltistan, Diamir and Gilgit) is 84,253,644. The constitution of Pakistan envisages an Islamic state. Muslims constitute about 97 per cent of the total population, the remaining being mainly the Hindus and the Christians (Grover 1997).

Since time immemorial, there has been migrations of a number of groups from Central Asia, Asia Minor, Turkmenistan and Armenia to Pakistan. Some of them were mainly Aryan or mixed Aryan and Mongol stock, beside some groups from western Asia, on a smaller scale. The people who built the Indus Valley Civilisation seems to be Dravidians who differed in physical appearance, culture and languages from the latter arriving Aryans. (Qureshi 1976). All these elements have mixed in varying degrees in different parts of Pakistan, although the dominant group is Indo-Aryan.

History of Migration

In Pakistan, the Indus Valley Civilisation flourished with its centre at Mohenjo-Daro, in the district of Larkana, Sind. The

Aryan called entire area of Sind, Punjab, Kashmir and east Afganistan as *Sapta Sindhu*, the land of seven rivers and the north-west part of India as Sinda.

The dawn of history began with the Aryan dynasty in power. After that several ethnic transmissions like the Persian, Greek, Mauryan, Scythian, Arabian and lastly the British occurred during different period of time. Thus contribution of different genetic components and diffusion of various cultures had been set forth. The arterial routes of the Indus attracted traders and invaders from the Arabian Sea. Traffickers from Palmyra and Alexandria had come that way to meet the caravans of High Asia. Centuries earlier ships may have passed that way from the prehistoric cities of the Indus to the proto-historic cities of Sumer, as later they sailed to the ports of Babylon. Arabs had come that way for temporal benefit in Sind and Punjab. The passes of Baluchistan and the western Himalayas had borne the existence of the prehistoric villagers, Turkmenistan caravans, Aryan, Greek, Afghan, Mughul and Iranian invaders along the other familiar channels where nature has cut between plateau and plain. Some of these invaders had lingered in the great valley of the Indus and its tributaries, others had passed on eastwards to expand to north India, to be absorbed ultimately in a greater vastness than human effort could encompass (Wheeler 1950). The primary direction of the gene flow of the Indo-Aryan speakers of the lowland hill tribes has been from west to east, but periodically in the past there might have been an opposite trend. In Afganistan and Baluchistan the permanent colonies of plain Gujars were dated from the Kushan and other from the Gupta times. Biologically a higher degree of endogamy existed among the hill tribes than the people of plains. The process of miscegenation and migration have taken place in the past. Islam reached the Indus basin through Arabs and a mixed array of Turks and Iranians at a later stage. In neolithic times the Brahui, the Dravidian outlier or Turko-Mongol, largely isolated for possibly four millenia might have been connected with Zhob and Lora valleys and the Khej river site in Makran coast. It was probably through the Gaj river route to the lake of fish (Manchhar), near Amri, the first settler from the plateau to the plains settled. The Brahui, who straddle the Baluchi-Afghan border, were divided into three territorial sections, each section was subdivided into six to twelve sub-sections. The major section practised nomadic and sedentary agriculture. Settled or migratory smiths, carpenters and other craftsmen speaking Pusto, Sindhi and Jatki served the local communities. Most of the names of the sub-sections are recognised as Brahui Dravidian, like Saka, Lari, Luri, Jatak, Kurd, Gujar, Sunar etc. Admixture of such groups with Iranian and Turks seems to be clear.

The coastal fishing communities of Las Bela are most complex. They carry genetic traces ranging from east African Negroids and south coastal Arabs to the Laskars of Gujarat and the Malayali Dravidian of Malabar.

The northern half of the Suleiman sector was inhabited by Ghilzai and nomadic plateau Pathans such as the Pani and Luri, in the southern half Baluchis - the Marri, Bugti, Mombki and Khetrani and several minor sub-tribes. The Baluchis, those are identified with the Parthians have a tradition of north Iranian origin and of residence in Seistan until about the 1000 A.D. During the next half a millenium, their migrations were traced in two directions, one southern into Makran and other coastward into lower Suleiman and the adjacent plains of the Sind. The ethnic complexity of the Baluchis of Pakistan has probably been for thousand of years. The west Baluchistan has a sparse population of tent-dwellers.

Contrasting with the hill tribes of Iranian plateau border, the Punjabis and the Sindhis of the western plain of Pakistan merge imperceptibly with the inhabitants of the eastern

Punjab. Throughout, the entire Sindhi-Punjabi speaking group forms a largest single socially distinct group as *Jati*. The Jats, irrespective of different religious groups, accounts for twenty-five percent of the population, nearly three times that of the Rajputs. Formerly, the Rajputs, Jats, Gujars, Arains, Khatris, the Meos were classified as tribal castes.

Population

The dominant population in the four provinces of Pakistan are (i) the Punjabis of Punjab, (ii) the Sindhis of Sind, (iii) the Pustuns of North Western Frontier Province and (iv) the Baluchis (Pathan) of Baluchistan. Besides there are others like (v) the Mahajars or Muhajirs, the urdu-speaking refugees from India, they consist of fifty per cent of Sind population residing in the urban areas, (vi) the Makranis of Baluchistan and (vii) the Khas and the Kafirs of Chitral residing in the northern area, Gilgit, Baltistan etc.

Bowels (1977) described that, though the hominid or human remains of palaeolithic period are not found in the area, but thousands of artefacts from numerous sites point to probable contact and migration either westward or eastward or both direction during all major prehistoric periods. The historic trend of migration from north and west to south and east has been the traditional pattern characterising human society in Pakistan. The hilly region preserve continuity in the archaeological entity.

The earliest human inhabitants of Pakistan are represented by crudely-chipped stone tools, which occupy an important place in the archaeology of Asia (pre Sohan) as implements of natural origin. The late Sohan tools are treated as combination of an intrusive Levalloiso-Mousterian elements and a pebble tool tradition (Stiles 1978). The lower palaeolithic findings in Jhelum district of Punjab were the earliest type in Pakistan as well as in whole of South Asia.

Dani (1964) established a new Stone Age sequence in North-West Frontier Agency into three phases. The middle and upper palaeolithic phases were found in several sites in Sind (Allchin 1976). In Mehrgarh most characteristic tools are borers and geometric microliths such as, lunates, triangles, trapezes etc. The microlithic flint industry shared a common trait with late Stone Age of India but the presence of turquoise and Lapis Lazuli denote the long distance contact, probably with West and Central Asia. In Sohan region, stone tools along with chopper and hand axe bear resemblance to Madras industry of south India as found in Acheulian of Europe, Arab and Africa. Recently Stone Age culture defined by British team in Pothware region opened a path to continuous process of development from lower to upper palaeolithic period. Primitive folks from the river side of Punjab (Hunters and food gatherers) used chopper and hand axes. Before five thousand years, herdsmen and farmers lived in primitive village in the little valley of hill and river side having limited contact with their other neighbours.

During mesolithic period, scattered by hunting and gathering, man was living in the alluvial plains, marshy lands and open parklands of the major villages located on the banks of river. Coastal and inland trade routes connected these mesolithic communities with Iran and South-East Asia.

India apparently derived much of its neolithic as well as metal age civilisation from Makran coast and Baluchistan in the west. But the process of food producing economy and village formation was a revolutionary discovery, excavated by the French Archaeological Mission at Mehrgarh in Baluchistan. This process culminated in the gradual development of first urban settlement in Pakistan.

The cultural area like Kulli, Nal, Zhob, Lora and other valleys of south Suleiman complex had no direct connection with the culture of the plains. Pottery discovered in south

Baluchistan (Quetta, Amri, Nal and Kulli) was of buffware culture whereas redware culture was found in Zhob of north Baluchistan. The culture of Kulli had shown more closeness to the Indus civilisation in figures and seals. In Nal, 'excarnation', i.e. removal of flesh from cemetry, shows similarity with the custom practised by the Parsis.

Indus Valley Civilisation was the final product of a long history and not an isolated development. Both rise and fall in these civilisation represented a complicated phenomenon of human development. The post Indus development was enriched by new material as found in Pirak, Taxilla, Aligrama and a large number of burials widely scattered in the northern part of Pakistan.

Robert Bruce Foote (1916) described that celadon ware, a very peculiar type of pottery which is found largely from Karachi to Babylon and from China to Arabia, appears to have reached Makran long after migration of Brahui that reached south India. He also suggested that Dravidian immigration into India by Makran coast was from Asiatic highlands to borderland of India. Some of them remained for centuries either on the coast line, where they built strange dwelling and buried the dead in earthen pots or they were entangled in the mass of frontier hills which lacked the solid Kirthar. That area was inhabited by a Turko-Mongol race, the Brahui (men of the hills). The Dravidian overlaid them and by intermixing preserved the Dravidian language but lost the Dravidian characters.

The megalithic graves of Waghodur, twenty miles east from Karachi, exactly resemble those found in the Deccan and the Nilgiri in India, except for the hole in one side of the stone or wall. H.B.E. Frere, the then Commissioner of the Sind (cited by Wheeler 1950) added that:

> Cairness and Cromlechs, such as are described by Taylor, are common on the road to Shah Billawal in Baluchistan and

also in the hills on the direct road from Karachi to Kotri. They are generally known as Kafir graves.

This term implies the tradition of pre-Muslim origin.

Table 3 : Groups Present in Pakistan and India

Group	Pakistan	India
Mediterranean	Punjab (Punjabi Chhetris of Lahore) and Sind	Punjab, Uttar Pradesh and Rajasthan (Rajput Banias)
Brachycephalic	Baluchistan - Sind	Himalaya to south India
Alpine	Baluchistan (Brahui) and Sind (Brahui)	Gujarat (Banias), Kathiawar (Kathi), Bengal (Kayasthas)
Dinaric	Burushaski speaking Pathans	Bengal, Orissa, Karnataka (Mysore Brahmins)
Armenoid	Parsis	Gujarat (Parsis), Maharashtra (Parsis)
Nordic	Kafirstan (Red Kaffirs, Kalas and Pathans) Chhetris of Lahore (mixed with Mediterranean) Pathans of N.W. Frontier and Peshawar (mixed with Oriental Dinaric)	Punjab, Kashmir (Kashmiri Brahmins and Muslims), Maharashtra (Chitpavan Brahmins), Gujarat (Nagar Brahmins)

Biological Affinities

The mediterranean characters like long head and face, long concave nose, tall stature are strongest among the populations of undivided Punjab, Sind, Rajputana (now Rajasthan) and western Uttar Pradesh. These features are common among the Rajput Banias, Punjabi Chhetris of Lahore and others. Other important racial elements like western brachycephals having broad head, more specifically Alpine, Dinaric and

Armenoid can be traced in south Baluchistan and Sind which are also dominant characters in most of the people in several states of India. Guha (1931) observed the distribution of brachycephalic people from Himalayan region to south India and found maximum frequency in Pamir, Baluchistan, Afganistan and Sind region of Pakistan. Alpine groups bearing broad and round head, round face, medium stature, light complexion, presence of body hair are observed among the Brahuis of Baluchistan, Banias of Gujarat, Kathis of Kathiawar and Bengali Kayasthas of undivided Bengal. Round and broad head, long head, long and concave nose, long face, tall stature and slightly darker complexion are the Dinaric characters which are observed among the people of Bengal, Orissa, Coorg, Brahmins of Mysore and Burushaski speaking Pathan group of Pakistan. Armenoid characters like broad head, thin and parrot-beak nose, light-yellowish complexion, short to medium height are found among the Parsis of Pakistan and of Gujarat and Maharashtra region of India. Nordic came from north-east corner of undivided India and settled in Punjab and Kashmir. Their characteristic features are long head and face, short nose, high nasal bridge, protruding occiput, light complexion, arched forehead, medium to tall stature, stout body and blue or grey eyes. The Red Kaffirs of Kafiristan, the Kalas and Pathans of Pakistan and the Chitpavan Brahmins of Maharashtra are the example of Nordic.

Bhalla (1989) also observed that the Nordic element is associated with the Vedic Aryans who swept into India as the last great movement of people from the west. This type is most conspicious among the Pathan tribes of North-Western Frontier of Pakistan, mixed with oriental and Dinaric elements. In Punjab and Rajputana and among the upper classes of northern India, it is also present but of increasing admixture with older mediterranean elements. It is traceable among the Pathans and Chhetris of Lahore and in western India (Nagar Brahmins) mixed with broad-headed people and as far as undivided Bengal.

From the ancient skeletal remains S.S.Sarkar (1969) assesed that Harappa and Adittanalur crania are of common ethnic strain. Kennedy (1984) put forward an interesting observation which reads:

> When multivariate studies are made using data from population of the Mediterranean, western Asia and the area influenced by the ancient Harappa in south Asia, a biological continuum extending over some five millennia is demonstrable. In short, the ancient Harappa are not markedly different in their skeletal biology from the present day inhabitants of north-western India and Pakistan, which in turn, share a high frequency of phenotypic characters with both ancient and living peoples of Afganistan, Iran and the land bordering of Aegean and Mediterranean.

A.K. Kalla (1994) also observed by comparing the populations of Sind and Baluchistan with the western Indians that the tribals as well as the non-tribals of Sind and Baluchistan are more tall, broad headed and long nosed than the respective populations of western India. According to him this is reasonably expected as Guha's assumption that the tall statured, broad headed and longer nosed Alpino-dinaric element which has contributed both to the non-tribal and the tribal populations of India, reached western India through Baluchistan and Sind. The evidence of skeletal biology indicates that the Harappans in Punjab and Sind resembled present day Punjabis, Sindhis and Gujaratis, (Dhavalikar 1995). This has also been observed by Sarkar (1968).

Serological studies among the populations of Pakistan is not adequate enough so as to enable to draw a comprehensive picture regarding biological relationships of the populations of India and Pakistan. However, from the available records it is observed that there is a high frequency of B gene among the Pathans of Dir, Multan, Peshawar and Swat; Muslims and Urdu-speaking group of Karachi, Quetta and Peshawar; the Punjabis of north Pakistan, Lahore, Rawalpindi and Quetta and among the Rajputs of Quetta. Similar trend has also been reported among the Dogras, Gujars, Rajputs, Jats, Kshatris, Aroras, Makrani Muslims, Marathis, Kokonanastha Brahmins, Lad Vanias, Ladakis and the Kashmiri Muslims of India. It is interesting to note that the population of India which has been referred to above, are distributed in north-western and western parts of Indian subcontinent, which is adjacent to Pakistan. Mourant and others (1976) have also reported the similar features and observed that the frequency of B gene increases from west Pakistan to northern and central India, which they ascribed as a response to environment as well as impact of natural selection acting over last four thousand years.

High frequency of MS gene is a typical Caucasoid character, similar to Arab. In west Pakistan and Gujarat, it is below 65 per cent, but in northern and north-eastern India it is more than 70 per cent. S gene is found to be slightly above 30 per cent in west Pakistan and northern India. In west Pakistan Rh frequencies scarcely differ from those of typical Mediterranean populations (Caucasoid) with 55 per cent of $CDe(R_1)$ and 25 percent cde(r). The Muslim and the Brahmins of western and northern India tend to show lower $CDe(R_1)$ and higher cde(r) charcters. In Pakistan, the Baltis, Hunzas and the Pathans possess below 50 per cent P gene, whereas in the adjacent areas of Pakistan, the Koli and Naika of Gujarat, Chandra Seniya Kayastha Prabhu, Kokanastha and Chitpavan Brahmin of Maharashtra possess above 50 per cent of P gene.

Besides blood groups, there have been some studies on red-cell enzymes, particularly G6PD deficiency undertaken among a few populations of west Pakistan. In India a number of studies have been conducted on G6PD deficiency. But for the present exercise we will consider that population of western India, which is closer or contiguous to Pakistan. The Pathans in west Pakistan possess as high as 7.89 and 4.71 per cent of G6PD deficiency (Stern et al. 1968, Ronald et al. 1968) followed by the Punjabis (Ronald et al. 1968, McCurdy and Mahmood 1970) and 3.57 per cent among other Pathans and Punjabis (McCurdy and Mahmood 1970). A closer look on the data from Indian subcontinent reveals that the deficiency of G6PD is relatively higher among a section of northern and western India. The highest frequency of G6PD deficiency was reported (Agarwal et al. 1974, Kate et al. 1974, Mourant et al. 1976) among the Sindhis (20 per cent), followed by the Khatris (14 percent), Kutchi Banshalias (13 per cent), Mahars (10 per cent), Audich Brahmins (3.55 per cent) and the Lohanas (3 per cent).

Cavilli-Sforza (1994) while trying to understand the genetic relationship of the populations of southern Asia has observed that there is a sub-cluster comprising of ten Indo-European groups spread over many countries, including India and Pakistan. This signifies closer resemblance of biological relationship of the populations of India and Pakistan.

Conclusion

In sum, it is observed that an appraisal of the paths of migration both in modern and ancient times, establish the existence of admixture between the people of both migrants and local identified group. The discussion in pre pages brings one very important aspect into relief. In order to understand the biological affinities, the knowledge about the cultural diffusion and linguistic exchange is also important besides the information on the genetic aspects of the populations.

Biological Affinities of the Populations of Nepal, Bhutan and Bangladesh with Those of India

J.M. Sarkar

Introduction

Biological affinities between people of a country or some countries suggest existence of probable miscegenation of these people. Extent of such admixture between the population of India with those of Bangladesh, Bhutan and Nepal, which are situated in geographical proximity, is discernable from their morphological and sero-genetic affinities or variations.

Nepal

Nepal is somewhat rectangular in shape and is located along the southern flank of the Himalayas. It is surrounded by India on the east, west and south and by China on the north. According to popular legend, the name Nepal is derived from the name of a celebrated ascetic called Ne who cherished or looked after the land. From the fourth century A.D. upto mid eighteenth century various parts of Nepal were ruled by the Hindu dynasty and other rulers. The modern nation of Nepal was established in 1769 by Shri Prithwi Narayan Shah.

Between 1985 and 1993, German Research Council alongwith the Department of Geology and Archaeology of Tribhuban University of Nepal excavated various prehistoric sites in the south western part of Nepal. On the basis of this, a German archaeologist, Gudrun Corvinus (1994) was of the opinion that Nepal was occupied by prehistoric populations from early paleolithic times onwards. She added that the Himalayas formed the northern boundary of the extension of the classical handaxe culture of the African and Indian tradition. In eastern Nepal the mesolithic industry is unique in lithic expression and indicating the possible affinities with South-East Asia via north-east India.

The bio-cultural relation between Nepal and India could be traced from the epic age. It is mentioned in the Ramayaña that Sita, the daughter of the king Janak of Nepal, was married to Rama – the prince of Ayodhya (India). During the period of the Mahabharata, a Kiranti / Kirati king of Nepal took the side of Pandavas against the war with the Kauravas. Many ruling dynasties of Nepal like the Mauryas, the Lichchavis, the Thakuris, the Kirantis, the Mallas, the Shahs were the immigrants to Nepal from the plains of India. On the other hand many religious personalities like Kashyapa Muni, Kanaka, Sikhi Buddha and others came with their followers to Nepal via India and blended Buddhism and Hinduism with the local religion.

Population

From the ancient records it seems that Nepal was originally inhabited by the Mongoloid people. B.H. Hodgson (1847) concluded that the Nepalese are of Tibetan origin and his observation was based on three main reasons, such as the physiognomy of the Nepalese is of Mongolian type which is the characteristic feature of the Tibetans, the evidences of comparative vocabularies and the creeds, and, customs and legends of the Nepalese conform to the same conclusion. Their legends indicate a transit of the Himalayans from thirty-five to fourty-five generations back. The transit was certainly made before the Tibetans who had adopted the religion and literature of the Buddhist from India in the seventh and eighth century A.D.

According to Hodgson (1847) the earliest inhabitants of Nepal were the Chepangs, the Kusundas and the Mayas. Their number was very small like some of the primitive tribes of India. Their dialect seems to be similar to the Munda and the other Kolarian languages found in India. They belong to Proto-Australoid groups who inhabited the Indian mainland from early times.

Another indigenous inhabitants of Nepal are the Newars who bear physical features of Mongoloid and Mediterranean type. They are bilingual and speak both Nepali (Indo Aryan language) and Newari (Tibeto-Burman language). B.D. Sanyal (1947-48) and Gopal Singh Nepali (1965) concluded that the Newars might have originated in south India, with distinct similarities with the Nairs of Malabar coast. But this affiliation appears to be cultural rather than somatological.

The Khas and the Kiraties are another ancient people of Nepal. Historical record shows that a group of Khas shepherds belonging to Aryan stock, had settled in western Nepal. The Khas spoke a language allied to Sanskrit and were a people akin to the brahmins. According to Sanyal:

> The Khas are in fact the back bone of the Himalayan populations. They might be called Khasia Rajput in Kumaon and Gorkhas in Nepal. The Khas blood is more mixed with Kshatriya blood from India than elsewhere in Nepal.

The Kiratas or Kirantas are referred to in the Mahabharata as the dwellers of the north-eastern Himalayas. A religious book like *Kirant Ko Veda* (Chemjong 1961) maintained that "at least some of Kirant ancestors and ancient Rajas came from Tibet. They speak in Tibeto-Burman dialect. They look like Mongoloid with pale yellowish pigmentation and flat faces with almond shaped eyes". Communities like the Rais and the Limbus are supposed to be the representatives of this group. Another interesting community is known as Satar who are believed to be the same people as the Santhals of Bihar taking into consideration their clan names and religious cult.

According to 1991 Census (Grover 1997), the total population of Nepal was 18,462,081. There are many distinct and diverse peoples living in this country. The Tarai region is populated mainly by the Maitheli Brahmins, Rajputs, Bhuinyars, Kurmis, Telis, Tharus, Danwars, Rajbanshis, Satars and the Musalmans. The hilly region is mainly inhabited by the Newars, Rais, Limbus, Tamangs, Mangars, Gurungs, Thakuries, Brahmins and the Chhetris. The Sherpas, Lhomis and the Lepchas live in the northern region. A.C. Sinha (1975) classified the Nepalese population into four broad social groups such as, (1) Kiranti/Kirati (Rai, Limbu, Lepcha, Tamang) found in north-eastern and eastern part of Nepal, (2) Newars inhabit in Kathmandu valley and eastern Nepal, (3) Thakuries or Gurkhali Khas – who are the counterparts of the Indian Hindu endogamous caste and (4) the Chhetris found in all parts of Nepal.

Migration

In Nepal there was continuous wave of immigrants from the north, south and west during the Mughal invasion (1526 A.D.). There was large influx of the Hindus into Nepal. Indian influence was at the peak during the reign of Kushanas and Guptas in India. During thirteenth century, Mallas from south India established their dynasty in Nepal.

Karan et al. (1963) observed that Nepal was populated mainly by large-scale migrations over a period of many centuries from all the surrounding areas. The intermixture of Mongoloid groups from Tibet with Indo-Aryan people from northern India has gone far to break down homogeneity of race, in the strict sense. B.L. Joshi and L.E. Rose (1966) noted that most of the populations of Nepal were composed of Indo-Aryan migrants from the plain and hilly areas of northern India. The Brahmins and the Rajputs migrated from India to Nepal through the south-western side. The Kshatriyas of Nepal trace their origin through the Surya and Chandra Vanshi Rajas of Udaipur and other Rajputana states. The Muslims came to Nepal from Kashmir and Uttar Pradesh as traders and refugees during the reign of Ratnamalla (1484 to 1520 A.D.). Various historical accounts revealed that the emigration began after 1850 and much of it was across the border into Sikkim, Bengal, Assam, Bhutan and Burma (Nakane 1966). L. Caplan (1970) has noted that by 1891 about half of the population of Darjeeling was of Nepalese origin. Thus, on the basis of migration of the people of Nepal it is presumed that some Mongolian element might have been introduced from Tibet into Nepal from the north via Sikkim. On the other hand some Indo-Aryan strains were introduced through south-west of Nepal.

Biological Relationship

B.D. Sanyal (1947-48) is of the opinion that "geography has introduced Tibetan blood into Nepal from north and via Sikkim and history has send streams after streams of Hindustani fugitives into the different valleys, mainly from the south west. As a result of these processes, Tibetan blood is predominant in the north and east of Nepal and the Indo-Aryan blood distinct from that of earlier Nepal in the valleys of Karnauli and Rapti, while some other parts of Nepal preserved to a certain extent the racial complexion that they did have about 1000 B.C."

No systematic physical anthropological study among the people of Nepal has so far been done. But some authors like Herbert Risley (1915), Bird et al. (1957), Horrobin et al. (1976), W.T. Agar (1946), M.K. Bhasin (1970) etc have done some work among the Nepalese population. It is true that some castes and tribes are found both in India and Nepal having common physical features. Communities like the Bhoksas, Tharus, Sherpas, Lepchas, Bhotias, Newars, Limbus, Sunwars, Rais, Khas etc. are to be found both in India and Nepal. According to Risley, the Nepalese are "mesorrhine, platytopic and brachycephalic with low or medium stature, sturdy build, yellowish complexion, broad face and low facial angle". Both the Tharus and Bhoksas have Mongoloid affinities which are characteristic features of Nepal and north-eastern population of India.

Regarding the blood group study in Nepal and India, it is observed that there is a biological relationship between the populations of the two countries. Bird and other studied the Gorkhas of Nepal and observed that the frequency of A gene (42.5%) is higher than that of B (20.0%). Similarly A gene is also higher than B gene among the tribal populations of north-eastern India such as the Khasis (19.20)%, Galongs (21.58%), Noctes (21.84%), Padams (25.00%), Pasis (36.02%), Lepchas (21.9%). T.T. Tanaka Miki (1960), N.Kumar, B.M. Das (1969), P.N. Bhattacharjee (1954, 1957). Bird et al. (1957), Horrobin et. al. (unpublished) and Bhasin (1970) reported that the gene A_2 present among the Gorkhas and the Newars, is also found among most of the Indians. Bird et al. (1957) reported that the total M gene (70.25%) of the Gorkhas of Nepal is similar to some of the Indian populations. Srivastava (1965) also observed that the gene M (72.93%) of the Tharus bear a closer resemblance to the Gorkhas of Nepal.

Bhutan

Bhutan, a kingdom in the Himalayas with an approximate area of 18000 square miles is divided into three main geographical areas. The northern Bhutan lies within the great Himalayas while the middle region contains several fertile valleys. Along the southern border of Bhutan lies the Doars plain which extend into India. The name Bhutan has been derived from the Sanskrit word *Bhotanta* i.e., end of Tibet. It has come from the conjunction of the words '*Bhota*' and '*Anta*' (Chakrabarti 1979).

The early history of Bhutan is enveloped in darkness because most of the ancient records had been destroyed due to flood, earthquake, fire and internecine wars. The most remarkable example of this destruction is the burning of Poonakha in 1832 and widespread destruction of buildings due to earthquake of 1897. However, White (1971) made an attempt to gather historical information of Bhutan on the basis of available ancient records. According to earliest legend as reported by White, Sangladip emerging from the environs of Kooch subdued the land of Bengal and Bihar sometime about seventh century B.C. The famous Indian Buddhist monk, Padmasambhava from Nalanda, visited Bhutan and converted the original inhabitants to Buddhism. The old Tibetan manuscripts indicate that the relation of Bhutan with Tibet was very close in terms of religion and culture. Historically Bhutan maintains intimate ties with Sikkim as well as Nepal.

Bhutan became a separate political entity some three hundred years ago when a Tibetan Lama named Sheptoon Lapha proclaimed himself as a king. Subsequently the land was ruled by two leaders, a Dharmaraja for spiritual matters and a Devraja for political and administrative affairs. The hereditary line of ruling dynasty was established by the governor of Tongsa in eastern Bhutan in 1907 aided by the

British. The king is assisted by an advisory council of civil servants and Buddhist leader while there exists a national assembly directly elected by the people. L.E. Rose (1977) observed that the population of Bhutan consisted of four distinct groups, such as (a) Tibetan migrants during early part of ninth century (b) Indo-Mongoloid group of people who migrated from Assam to eastern Bhutan during last millenium (c) Indigenous tribal groups namely the Drokpas, the Lepchas and (d) Nepalis migrants residing in Bhutan for about three to four generations.

White (1971) categorised the population of Bhutan into those living in the east and those living in the west. According to him the population living in the east are having short stature, dark complexion and finner physical features as compared to those living in the west. The western Bhutanese though profess Buddhism but are not so rigid about their customs. The people of the west are mostly of Tibetan origin who inhabit the country since the last few centuries. They are tall having a well-developed body build and fair complexion.

The Mons and the Khens are said to be the earliest inhabitants of Bhutan. The Mons are distributed in the eastern end of the Brahmaputra valley, Bhutan, China, India to north-west Burma. The Shar Mon, a section among them, inhabiting the Kameng district of Arunachal Pradesh and eastern Bhutan are considered the earliest settlers of the region (Sinha 1991). He referred the Kirati (Rai, Limbu) tribes in Sikkim as the Mons. There were different tribes such as the Kiratis and Hindus who are living between Tibet and Indian plains like Ladakh, Kulu, Nepal, Sikkim, Bhutan, Arunachal Pradesh and Paldo known as Mon by Tibetan who did not profess lamaism and lived by hunting.

Khen is another ancient community in Bhutan. They speak in Austric language, which is frequently referred to as related to Koch, Bodo and even to the Khasi tribe of Meghalaya. According to Sinha (1991), they represent a very ancient survival, who once upon a time, provided the intermediary relationship between Tibet on one side and Assam and Bengal on another and this community has a distinct Indo-Mongoloid affinity. Beside these there are communities like the Bhotias, Doyas, Birmis (Nomadic), Mechs, Kochs, Kacharis, the Rajbansis etc., living in Bhutan. Both the Bhotias and the Birmis are of Tibetan origin and they have their own customs and languages.

According to official record of 1990, the population of Bhutan was estimated at 1.6 millions (Grover 1997). Among them 30 to 35 per cent are Nepalese who reside in south Bhutan. These Nepalese migrated to Bhutan from Nepal or Sikkim and Darjeeling about a century ago. The Nepalese are the Gorkhas, Limbus, Rais, Gurungs, Damais, etc. There are some people who migrated from Uttar Pradesh, Punjab, Bihar, and Rajasthan as wage labourers, merchants, peasants, shopkeepers and officials in the recent past.

No systematic physical anthropological work has been done among the Bhutanese in Bhutan. Most of the works are based on regional study rather than on social groups. Anthropometric study has been done by Risley and Tiwari among the Bhutanese, Kirantis and Lepchas but on a very small scale. Both the Kiranties and the Lepchas are short statured and broad headed, where as Bhutanese are medium statured with broad and medium nose.

Serological studies have been done by Glassgow and others, (1968) and Mourant et al. (1968) in Bhutan. According to Mourant et al., the people of Bhutan are more Mongoloid in their blood group gene frequencies. Both Glasgow and Mourant observed that there is high frequency of B gene (48 %) among the Bhutanese which is the characteristic of most of the Indian population. Similarly, M gene (54.5 %) is high among the Bhutanese population which are also found among the Indian population, like the Riangs (89 %) of Tripura (Kumar and Sastry, 1961) and the Noctes (80 %) of Tirap Frontier Division (Bhattacharya 1957).

Relatively low MS gene and absence of CDE appear to be the characteristic features of the Bhutanese as observed among the population of north-east India.

The Mongoloid populations are characterised to have Di-a (Diago) antigen which is found among the Bhutanese as it is reported for the Rajbansis of Koch Bihar (West Bengal). Besides, higher frequency of Fy (a+) antigen which is a Mongoloid characteristic is also found among the Bhutanese and Rajbansis.

Bangladesh

Bangladesh is one of the youngest nation though it has a long history. Bangladesh, a free independent country emerged in 1971 after it got liberated from Pakistan. Prior to that it was known as East Pakistan under the control of Pakistani administration. Bangladesh is bounded on three sides by India having Burma in south-east and Bay of Bengal in the south.

The early history of Bangladesh is obscure. It is popularly believed that around 1000 B.C. the Bang tribe, an offshoot of Dravidian, was pushed out of the upper Ganges valley by the Indo-Aryans and the territory thus populated by the Bang came to be known as Bengal. During the third century B.C. the Maurya empire occupied the territory and encouraged the propagation of Buddhism under the rule of Emperor Ashoka. Later on it came under the control of Gupta empire. During ninth century A.D. Pala dynasty came into power before it was taken over by the Muslim ruler. It became a part of British rule till 1947 when the territory was annexed to Pakistan and came to be known as East Pakistan. Subsequently, the land got independence in 1971 and the nation, Bangladesh, was established. Bangladesh thus experienced waves of domination of different people who made an impact on the life and culture of its population. The prehistoric information on Bangladesh is much scanty. There are reports on two prehistoric sites. Chakraborti (1992) discovered the fossil wood industry of palaeolithic period in the Lalmai hills of the Comilla district which he compared with the similar palaeolithic artifacts found in Chota Nagpur Plateau of Bihar and in Egara mile near Illambazar of Birbhum district of West Bengal. The other evidences of neolithic tools have been reported from the Sitakund hills of Chittagong represented by fossil wood shoulder celts (Banerjee 1321).

From the available material it is observed that the earliest people of Bangladesh were the Proto-Australoids. Most probably they entered from western Asia and spread over South-East Asia. They had dolichocephalic head, platyrrhine nose and dark brown complexion (Chatterjee 1952). This group most likely introduced agriculture into Bangladesh, which is supported by the distribution and type of artifacts as observed by E.C. Worman (1949). This hypothesis is also corroborated by the existence of Austric words in Bengali and related languages. They were probably followed from the east by a wave of Proto-Mongoloids, some of whom spread as far as the Chota Nagpur plateau. The main migration route of the Proto-Monglloids was however, towards South-East Asia. Soon, other elements were added to this melting pot.

The reference of the people of Bangladesh is found for the first time in the Brahmana and Aranyaka literature. The tribes like the Pundaras, Vangas and the Karvatas are quite often described. It may be surmised that the Pods (Pondrakshatriya) and the Kaibartas are the descendants of the Pundaras and the Karvatas respectively. Atul Sur (1963) is of the opinion that these two tribes along with the Bagdis are the oldest inhabitants of this territory. According to Subrata Banerjee (1981):

> Ethnically the Bangladeshi is a mixture of many races. The Austric or the Austro-Asians were the first to inhabit this territory in the prehistoric period, then came the Dravidians, Tibeto-Burmans, Aryans and Mongolians at different period of history. In the coastal regions of south Bangladesh traces of Arab blood can be found. Later on came the Turks, Pathans and Afghans. All of them left their mark on the physiognomy of the people who have distinct ethnic characteristics in different parts of the country.

According to 1981 Census, the total population of Bangladesh was 89.9 millions (Grover 1997). Out of this total population, eighty per cent of the people are composed of the Muslims, Hindus, Christians, Buddhists and the rest are tribals. The tribal populations are mainly concentrated in the hilly area of Bangladesh. Most of these populations are also found in India.

There are thirteen tribal groups in Chittagong hill tracts. They are the Chakmas, Marmas, Tipras, Tanchanyas, Mughs, Boms, Punkhos, Kukis, Mrus, Murangs, Riangs, Bonjogis and the Lushais etc. The Garos, Hajongs, Doluis, Hodis, Bundas, Khasias and Manipuris are also found in northern borders of the Mymonsing and Tangail districts and the north-east part of Sylhet of Bangladesh. Whereas the Oraons, Santhals, Rajbansis, Hos and Mundas etc. inhabit in the northern part of Bangladesh. On the basis of racial elements, Rashid (1977) classified the tribal populations of Bangladesh into three groups:

(1) Dravidian : The Oraons, who came from central India and settled in Bangladesh.

(2) Proto-Australoid : The Santhals and the Khasis are the two main tribes of this group. The Santhals migrated from Chota Nagpur plateau of India and settled in the

north-east district of Bangladesh since the 1870s. The Khasis came from the Khasi hills of the Meghalaya and settled in the Sylhet district of Bangladesh.

(3) The Mongoloid elements (with some Proto-Australoid admixture) : This group of tribal populations are mainly concentrated in the hilltracks of Chittagong district and are represented by the Kochs, Garos, Kacharis, Tipras, Chakmas, Mughs, Riangs, Mrus etc. The Kukis, Halems and Lushais live in north-east of Bangladesh, which is close to the state of Mizoram in India.

Biological Relationship

Very few physical anthropological studies have been done in Bangladesh. D.N. Majumdar (1950) studied the ABO blood groups among the Garos of undivided Bengal, where he found B gene is more than A gene. Attabudin (1954) has also done some work among the donors (1,000 samples) of Dhaka and reached a similar conclusion.

A comprehensive anthropometric study was conducted by D.N. Majumdar and C.R. Rao (1960) on sixty-seven social groups from twenty-nine districts covering West Bengal and the present Bangladesh in order to understand the biological relationship of different population groups living in this territory. On the basis of Cephalic Index (C.I.) they observed that the Muslims in general have a tendency towards brachycephalic head with the exception of the Muslims of Dinajpur, Khulna, Malda, Murshidabad and Rangpur who show dolichocephalic features. The value of C.I. is low among the tribals like, the Rajbanshis, Majhis, Mahatos etc. On the contrary the C.I. of the caste population (the Brahmins, the Kayasthas, the Mahisyas, the Baidyas, the Baishyas etc.) of undivided Bengal is comparatively high. The distance analysis (D^2) of the anthropometric data indicated that the tribals and the 'semi tribals' constitute a cluster, which is distinct from the cluster formed by the high castes.

Conclusion

The fore going discussion on socio-religious aspects reveals that the people of India, Nepal, Bangladesh and Bhutan have maintained intimate relationship among themselves from time immemorial. Socio-cultural linkages play the role of backbone of biological relationship. In spite of lack in availability of sufficient biological information, the preceding text speaks for the biological linkages among the people of these SAARC countries.

Part-II
Cultural Perspectives

Cultural Linkages Among the People of India, Sri Lanka, Nepal, Bhutan and Maldives

Jyotirmoy Chakraborty and
Rabiranjan Biswas

Through Trade

Trade is one of the important aspects of economic activities that helps in understanding the extent of cultural linkages, especially in case of ancient and medieval India. Trade was the means of contact with other people or societies through which the cultural elements had flown from one side to the other, as and when trade was regular and continuous. Evidences of trade are found in inscriptions, chronicles folk tales and other forms of literature.

The strategic position of India makes her eminently suited for maritime activities. The vast coastal line as well as wide network of navigable rivers have encouraged traders since ancient times. In search of acquiring wealth, the Indian traders and merchants explored unknown territories beyond their motherland across the seas and the mountains. Sometimes such endeavours were encouraged by the spirit of adventure of the Kshatriya princes and nobles. There are evidences of commercial interactions and interrelations which took place both through the land and the sea routes in the ancient historical past. R.C. Majumdar, H.C. Raychaudhuri and Kalikenkar Datta wrote that the activities of the sailors and the merchants were recorded in the Pali text though the date of such trade was not available (Majumdar et al. 1963). A careful study reveals that as early in the fourth century B.C. the municipal authorities of Pataliputra had to constitute a special board to supervise trade and commerce. Majumdar and others opined "a considerable portion of the state revenues came from traders... and the Maurya government built ships and let them out on hire for the transportation of merchandise" (Majumdar et al. 1963). The *Arthashastra* of Kautilya refers to shipbuilding activity during the Maurya period (c. 322-200 B.C.) The accounts of some foreign visitors also confirm that shipbuilding had reached a high degree of perfection around the fourth century B.C. Megasthenes stated that the shipbuilders used to receive their wages from the Maurya king (Chaudhuri 1986). In the writings of Pliny it appears that the sea between India and Taprobane (Sri Lanka) was not always of equal depth. Pliny also observes that some of the ships of the Maurya age had weighed about seventy-five tons (c.f. ibid 1986). Some references have been made in the indigenous literature like the *Chandimangala Kavya* composed by Kavi Mukundaram Chakraborty sometimes in the sixteenth century A.D. wherein a merchant of Ujani (present Ujjain) went for trade to Sri Lanka in the interest of the royal fund (Sen 1975). Benjamin Walker wrote that through out its long history, Ujjain was a meeting ground of nations from remote antiquity and it had maintained direct line of the great trade routes leading from the seaport of Barygaza (present Broach) and it was one of the most prolific centres of Indian culture (Walker 1968).

The archaeological evidences also suggest the existence of trade and trade routes of the past. The remains of a dockyard at Lothal is clearly an indication that the sea trade had existed even during the Indus Valley Civilisation. The arrival of the merchants and traders from India had been depicted in the ancient inscriptions of Ceylon (Law 1994). On the basis of archaeological evidences, Sri Lanka's foreign trade before 600 A.D. were in vogue with greater India and north India's contacts were visible from proto-historic to early and middle historic periods.

The discovery of ancient coins at different parts of South Asia also reveals trade relations between different countries. Singh wrote that the current archaeological finds help us to understand the importance of several places which played a dominant role in the trade relations in the Indian subcontinent with the outside world as well as internal trade. This has also been supported in early Indian literature. All this information help us immensely in depicting an outline of trade relations and trade routes during the early centuries of the Christian era(Singh 1988). He further wrote that both the rivers of western and southern India, Narmada and Kaveri, also played an important role in promoting the internal and international commerce of India. Developing an accurate idea of economic relationship of ancient and medieval India is not easy, as there are hardly any chronological references available on this particular aspect. However, some information available in the traveller's diary and incidental references from the legends, stories and chronicles helps in drawing some tentative picture of cultural linkages that once existed among the present countries of the SAARC viz., Sri Lanka, Maldives, Bhutan and Nepal.

The historical references suggest that three principal seaports were very much active in ancient India viz., Bhrigukachcha or Bharukachcha or Barygaza (present Broach), Surparakha or Sopara (near Mumbai) and Tamalitti or Tamralipti (present Tamluk). There are references of other smaller ports, one at Palura near Gopalpur (in Orissa) and three in southern part of India like Masulipatam, Calicot and Muciri, from where ships sailed across the Bay of Bengal to the Far East.

In *An Advanced history of India* R.C. Majumdar wrote that there was regular voyages from the mouth of the river Ganges along the eastern coast of India to Ceylon, and also along the western coast upto Broach at the mouth of the river Narmada. Generally the people of that time used to come through land or river routes to avail the nearest seaport. Majumdar also expressed "the existence of the trade routes between the eastern islands and the coast of Bengal, Orissa, Madras and Gujarat is established on good authority" (Majumdar et al. 1963). The author of *Masalik-ul-absar* wrote "merchants of all countries never cease to carry pure gold into India, and to bring back in exchange commodities of herbs and gums" (c.f. ibid 1963). According to Majumdar, "the ports of Bengal and Gujarat were then chiefly used for Indian export trade" (ibid). Further Barthema considered Bengal to be "the richest country in the world for cotton, ginger, sugar, grain and flesh of every kind" (cf ibid 1963). Interestingly, there are enough evidences of ancient traditions of Indian colonist in the Far East and South East Asia and constant flow of Indian emigrants to various parts of the world. The routes of migration of these Indians and the description of their journey towards their desired land have been mentioned in few legends and stories. According to the author of *Periplus of the Erythrian Sea*, Barygaza was the biggest centre of commerce in western India (Singh 1988). The most important port on the Malabar coast of Vijayanagar kingdom was Calicut through which commercial relation with the islands of the Indian Ocean was maintained. The main articles of export were cloth, rice, iron, sugar and spices. The commodities imported were mainly horses, elephants, pearls, copper, coral, mercury, silk and velvet. The overseas trade and commerce were run by the use of ships.

Trade with Ceylon/Sri Lanka

Ceylon or Sri Lanka was connected to India through trade because of its strategic position in the Indian Ocean. The Jaffna peninsula, which stretches up towards India into the Bay of Bengal, is separated from India by Palk Strait, a narrow shallow strip of water. The Coromandal Coast of India is less than twenty-five miles from northern Sri Lanka. Eratosthenes in his description of India wrote that there was seven days sail to reach Taprobane (Ceylon) from Coniaci (present Kanya Kumarika) (Sastri 1952). Owing to this favourable position for trade, there had been commercial relations with the neighbouring countries, from the very beginning of its history. Sinhalese memory goes to a time prior to the advent of Vijaya when trading vessels used to come to Ceylon in search of local products like ivory, wax, incense, pearls and gems. Wrecked ships on the shores of Ceylon were also found. Kosmos Indico-pleustes (535 A.D.), an Alexandrian monk, mentions Sri Lanka as a great resort of ships from all parts of India (cf Ray & Sen 1986). Ceylon was popularly known as Ratnadipa or land of gems among the mariners. This island was famous for gems and precious stones from very early times. All these gems were mostly available in the alluvial plains to the south-west of the Adams peak range of mountain. These gems were very famous for colour transparency or lustre. The most valuable gem of Ceylon was ruby, especially of pigeon-blood colour. The white and blue sapphires were other important gems of Ceylon. In the Gulf of Manner, it was found that at least some three hundred years before Christ there was abundant growth of pearl producing mussels locally called oyster. Wealthy merchants from the big towns of India and from Colombo used to go to buy pearls.

Ceylon also had internal trade. On the northern plains of Ceylon, trade routes had developed by the early first century A.D. There are references in the *Mahavamsa*, a Ceylonese chronicle, about a trader from Anuradhapura going to the hill country to bring ginger and other goods. Several inscriptions have also mentioned about such trade. In the *Mahavamsa* there are references of gifts sent by the king of Ceylon, Devanampiya Tissa to Emperor Ashoka. These were gems, pearl, diadem etc. along with insignia of royalty. The discovery of copper coins at Sigiriya and other archaeological sites clearly indicates that the internal trade was not confined to barter. Kosmos Indico-pleustes recorded that Ceylon was a key trading centre and because of its strategic position, the island was a great resort of ships from all parts of India, Persia and Ethiopia. The gold Kalanda coins of Ceylon were used for international trade and these coins were acceptable in south India. It may be mentioned here that Ceylon had to face greater competition from the Pandyans, the Cholas and the Arabs (De-Silva 1987). There are "epigraphic as well as literary references of trade relations with China, the Hellenic world, Ceylon and further India in the early centuries of the Christian era. These are recorded in the Nagarjunikonda inscriptions and the Milindapanho" (Majumdar et al. 1963).

Barthema, an Italian traveller, wrote that in 1505 when he visited Sri Lanka, the tanks were in disrepair and rice used to be imported from India (Cook 1951). In this context another reference as recorded by Willis says "the earlier pre-Sinhalese inhabitants must have had a very poor food supply, and in fact can hardly have been so well off as the Veddhas of today. Wijayo, the Sinhalese conqueror of 500 B.C., is said to have introduced rice from India which became national cultivation in course of timZe" (Willis 1907). K.M. De Silva, while describing the Aryan colonisation in Sri Lanka wrote that:

> There is for instance the possibility that traders reached the island while sailing down the Indian coast and that the natural products of Sri Lanka, in particular gems, may have provided the incentive for some of them to found settlement there
>
> (De Silva 1981)

However, such information of prehistoric time of Sri Lanka is mostly speculative as available in the travellers diaries and folk literature of this country.

While describing south India and Ceylon, K.A.N. Sastri wrote:

> Megasthenes had heard somewhat of the trade of the Sinhalese and of the polity of the Pandyan kingdom. He knows that Ceylon is an island more productive than India of gold and large pearls ...

(Sastri 1952). In support of his statement, Sastri quoted Kautilya who referred to the famous pearl Tamraparnika which was produced only in Tamrapani or Ceylon (ibid).

Trade with Maldives

In case of Maldives, information about trade is very limited. Only a few incidental references are available in the literature on Maldives. Unfortunately there is hardly any book on ancient and medieval Maldives. The Jataka tales suggest that the "seafarers emanating from Bharukaccha and Suppara visit the Maldives, but Gujaratis actually settled there in pre-Buddhist times" (Maloney 1980). Maloney mentioned on the basis of other Jataka tales that ships from Gujarat sailing for South-East Asia used to stop at Maldives and the merchants were in search of treasures from this island country. Perhaps the traders used to call it Mala-Div (ibid). The prehistoric information on Gujarat reveals that this land had maintained a tradition of early navigation over the past four thousand years or so, because of its vast coastal lines and its close proximity to the old navigation routes of Indus Valley Civilisation. The name Bharukachcha and Suppara, as ancient ports, have been mentioned in various ancient literature.

The central and southern ridges of Maldives are mostly ring like. The dangerous encircling reef, forming underwater walls, was a threat to the ancient mariners. Incident of shipwrecking has been described in several Jataka tales. Maloney is of the opinion "shipwrecked Gujaratis, as well as exiles, were early settlers on the northern islands of the Maldives group" (ibid). He also mentioned that mariners from the north-western coasts of the peninsula who commenced sailing to southern India, must have been in Maldives. The most important port on the Kerala coast at that time was Muciri, the Greeks called it Muziris. According to Ptolemy's list, the northern most port of Ariake is Suppara and there was regular trade between Gujarat and Kerala. Maloney wrote on the basis of Pyrad's observation that tortoise shell was largely exported to India from Maldives and there were only two sources for the tortoise shell – the Maldives and the Philippines (ibid 1980). These tortoise shells were marketed to Cambay (Khambat) and the shells were valued because these provide the plastic-like brown material used for curving bracelets, pendants, plaques, boxes, caskets lined with silver. These were fancy items of the Indian women. Tortoise shell was an important item of export of Maldives since early centuries of the Christian era (ibid 1980), prior to the conversion of the people of these islands into Islam (1153 A.D.) and even after the Tamils from south India had controlled much of the trade of Maldives.

In support of this fact, Maloney mentioned that many of the foreign ports as well as items of trade were known to the Divehi people by their Tamil names (ibid 1980). He further mentioned that the Pallavas and the Pandayas brought the Maldives into their trade networks. *Periplus of the Erythrian Sea* refers "the Cera kings controlled the sea routes and perhaps because the islands were peopled by south Indians" (cf. ibid 1980). Further Stefano, a Genoese merchant (1497) observed (referred to by Bell) "the people live on fish and a little rice, which they import" (cf. ibid 1980). He has not mentioned the place from where they used to import rice. Possibly they used to import rice either from India or from Ceylon. Wang Ta-Yuan (1330-49), a Chinese source describes (referred to by Nilkantha Sastri) "how a shipload of cowries from there (Maldives) buys a load of rice in Bengal" (cf Maloney 1980).

Another interesting information available in the writings of Edoardo Barbosa, who was present in India in 1516 A.D. describes "South India got its ship built in the Maldive islands. Epigraphic evidence proves that the rulers of Vijayanagar maintained fleets and the people there were acquainted with the art of ship-building before the advent of the Portuguese" (Majumdar et al. 1963). Barbosa also mentioned that Vijaynagar was highly populous and an active centre of commerce and the most important port on the Malabar coast was Calicut which maintained commercial relations with the islands in the Indian Ocean. Discovery of silver punch-marked coins in the relic caskets of Maldives, also found in the stupas, indicate wonderful clue on trade relation of Maldives. There are ancient symbol punched on the coins. These coins were used throughout South Asia even before the Mauryan times. Hence it could reasonably be presumed that Maldives was very much within the South Asian trade network during these centuries (Maloney 1980).

Trade between Maldives and Sri Lanka

Both Bell and Maloney opined that Maldivians had cultural affinity with Sinhala people. Like India, Sri Lanka had trade relation with Maldives in early part of the history. Maloney has given some reference of trade, "dried bonito has been the staple historic export of the Maldives and fish of Maldives is an important condiment in Sri Lanka and some neighbouring countries". De Silva also has given some reference of trade that the Maldives supplied to Sri Lanka with *kumbelamas* and cowries and took back in return spices, areca and some rice (De Silva 1981).

Trade with Bhutan

Besides the commercial relation with the outside world through sea route, India had trade relation through land routes with Central Asia, Afghanistan, Persia, Tibet and Bhutan (Majumdar et al. 1963). For a long time a large part of Bhutan was within the geographical and political boundaries of India. Hence the early relation between India and Bhutan was close and fascinating. The Sanskrit tradition refers that it was the Koch tribe who originally inhabited Bhutan (Ram Rahul 1971) and during the reign of King Ralpachen, the people of Tibetan origin arrived in Bhutan. Besides this, since ancient times Bhutan had constantly been in touch with Tibet and the people in the plains of Bengal and Assam. The cattle herders used to bring their sheep and cattle down to the plains in winter and also exchanged their butter. Both Bhutan and India had traditional ties of trade and commerce, as Bhutan was under the tutelege of Kamrupa Dynasty of ancient Assam. Ram Rahul wrote "in the past, Bhutan used to buy Indian areca-nut and silk and India was the market for Bhutanese ponies, musk and lac" (Ram Rahul 1971).

While discussing the modus operandi of trade flow between the eastern Himalayan subregion and Assam in the pre-colonial period, Ganguli wrote that there was a long tradition of brisk trade flow between Bhutan, Tibet, northeastern region of India and Assam. He further wrote that the 'duars' or the corridors served as the highway of commerce. Every winter, the traders from Bhutan, Tawang (Arunachal Pradesh) and the neighbouring areas used to come down to the foothills of Assam, through the Assam-Bhutan border. The items of exchange were mainly rock salt, gold dust, musk, woollen blankets, yaktails, ponies, etc against cloths, rawsilk, yarn, rice, dried fish and other items (Ganguly 1998). Some of the tribal communities acted as intermediaries between the different groups of traders.

Another dimension of trade relation according to Ram Rahul was a flourishing trade between India and Tibet and the Bhutanese acted as carrier agents. The Bhutanese used to collect dyes, endi (coarse silk) cloths, betel-nut and tobacco from India and in exchange they brought wool, salt and musk from Tibet (Ram Rahul 1971).

The Brokpas are the Bhutanese of Tibetan origin. Living in the high altitudes and tending cattle, yak, etc they follow semi-nomadic life for seasonal pastures. They carry on trade between eastern Bhutan and Tawang. It may be mentioned that there are some passages through the mountains, which facilitated the people inhabiting along the present political boundary to maintain linkages between the neighbouring countries. There are mountain passes like Dok-la and Jelo-la between Sikkim and Bhutan. The mountain passes like Sum-la, Sirkhim-la, Niengla, Gang-la maintained the linkages between the people of Bhutan and Arunachal Pradesh. All these mountain passes were mainly used for trade and for the spread of religion. Simultaneously, invasions also took place through these routes. Sinha mentioned that the present Kameng district of Arunachal Pradesh, traditionally known as Tawang tract was placed on the trade route between Kham

(Eastern Tibet) and Brahmaputra Valley (Sinha 1964). B. Chakravarti emphasised that "Bhutan had plenty of contact with her neighbours and the interesting point of the trade routes in the India – Bhutan – Tibet triangle was at Cooch Behar on the Indian plains" (Chakravarti 1979). Trade routes had existed in ancient and medieval Bhutan on the north with Tibet and on the south with India. The Bhutanese traders used to come as far as Jaigaon and Buzaduar for trade (Dorji et al. 1998). Such a flow of trade was stimulated by the needs of exchanging one group's surplus produces with those of the other group to meet their daily requirements. This trade relation promoted cultural exchanges, transmission of technology and learning of art and expansion of their world view too.

Trade with Nepal

The Himalayan kingdom of Nepal is very adjacent to the Indian subcontinent. Some parts of Nepal was under the Maurya emperor Ashoka of Magadh. From the very beginning it was influenced by the Indian subcontinent through migration of people, religious interactions and trade. There was ebb and flow of the people as recorded in the early history of Tarai region of Nepal. Around 900 B.C. the first Aryan tribesmen pushed eastward from the confluence of the Ganges and Yamuna and migrated to Tarai region. During this period (900 to 500 B.C.) the Aryans penetrated into the of present Uttar Pradesh and Bihar. They established the most powerful kingdom at Videha (Gaize 1975).

Tarai region of Nepal had more linkages with the greater Indian economic sphere than its own hilly regions. It emerged as the most productive region in the field of agriculture and industry, perhaps being stimulated by the economic activities of northern India. Exchange of agricultural produces were very common in those days.

During the reign of the Kirati kings in Nepal, trade flourished along with art and culture. Nepal became an important trade centre for the traders of India, Tibet and China, which strengthened the moral and material progress of the country (Thapa 1981).

The Lichchavis ruled Nepal from the beginning of the fifth century A.D. for about two hundred and fifty years. During this period, Nepal maintained an intimate relation with India and became more and more exposed to Indian commercial and cultural contacts. The Lichchavi kings introduced coinage system in Nepal for better transaction in trade and commerce. Ansuvarma, a defacto king of Lichchavi dynasty introduced copper and silver coins for commercial use. Gold coins were also introduced by the Lichchavi kings which benefited trade between India and Tibet.

Nepal was actively engaged in trans-Himalayan trade from the very early part of history between India and Tibet. Nepal acted as a bridge nation between the two countries. Nepal had transportation and communication through land routes with India and Tibet through the mountain passes and was dependent upon India for many essential commodities to a great extent. In the early part of the seventh century A.D. Tibetans appeared in the valley of Nepal after crossing the Kerong pass. They opened a more distinct route between India and China through Kathmandu valley. They also had access through Kashmir valley (Rose and Fisher 1970). The Tibetan goods like rocksalt, fur, herbs and drugs were sent down to Nepal via Kuti, Kerong Pass and Nuwakot and then all these items were exported to Indian market. Similarly the Nepalese and Indian commodities were imported to Tibet on the same route (Thapa 1981). The *T'-ang* chronicle of China mentioned that in the seventh and eighth centuries Nepal was very active and the country enjoyed almost a monopoly, especially on transit trade between Tibet and India. In the

Arthasastra the word Nepalakan (belonging to Nepal) denotes a special kind of rug made of sheep wool which was very popular in India (Varma 1972).

Items like gold, precious gems, musks, saffron and yak's tail were the chief objects of this long distance trade. The Chinese chronicle *T"-ang*, also mentioned that numerous merchants from India, Tibet and China used to assemble in the markets of Nepal. The *Mulasarvastivada Vinaya* (Tokyo edition chapter 21) tells us that some *bhikhus* (Buddhist monks) accompanied a group of traders proceeding to Nepal with hopes to visit the Buddhist shrines. The same Vinaya also mentions another story where a group of merchants of Sravasti was going to Nepal were joined by Buddhist pilgrims (ibid 1972).

During the period of the king of Karnata who ruled Nepal for about hundred and fifty years (1097-1245 A.D.) and even during the late medieval period, Nepal had intimate contact with northern Bihar and northern Uttar Pradesh which facilitated continuous interaction in the field of culture and commerce between the two countries.

Eastern India, especially Bengal and Bihar were popular centres of bronze casting. During the fifth and sixth centuries and particularly in the eighth century, many monks and priests went to Nepal from India carrying bronze images. Thus bronze metal craft penetrated in Nepal through these religious missionaries as well as trade and commerce (ibid 1972).

It is apparent from the above discussion on trade and trade routes of ancient and medieval period, that sea trade was much in vogue than the trade through land routes. The trade relation between India and Sri Lanka is antiquated, varied and continuous. Obviously there are sufficient and justified causes. Trade relations with Maldives were some how bipolar, from different parts of India like western, southern and eastern coasts on the one hand and from Sri Lanka, though very limited, on the other. Bhutan maintained its trade and commerce through the duars of Assam and Bengal and also through the mountain passes of Arunachal Pradesh and Sikkim. Bhutan also acted as carrier agent in the trade between India and Tibet. Role of Nepal in ancient and medieval trade network was primarily as a bridge nation between India and Tibet. However, the country also maintained some direct trade linkages through the Tarai region.

As the trade was regular and continuous, at least in some of the regions, there was a chance of a steady flow of Indian emigrants to various parts, leading to their settling down in those foreign lands permanently, as it happened in Sri Lanka and Nepal. This inconsistent but gradual penetration often added enthusiam to the missionaries who were active for the spread of religion, as apparent in case of Nepal and Sri Lanka. The fusion between the Indian settlers and the local inhabitants was complete even through the matrimonial alliances, to such an extent that in course of time it became difficult to distinguish between the two populations. Though all these legends and stories are not historically established, other references and evidences discussed here could not be ignored altogether.

Religious Linkages

Sri Lanka

Religion has played a great unifying role in the life and culture of the people of South Asia. The wide as well as diverse ethnic and linguistic composition, cultures and outlook on life, brought them to a common platform of intellectuals and spiritual personalities of the world. This also facilitated the medium of communication and exchange of ideas and culture among them. The religious dogmas, doctrines and movements enunciated by Buddhism, acquired the status of state religion after the conversion of Emperor Ashoka (250 B.C.). Various missions and emissaries were sent out for the spread of the new faith to different parts of the country and abroad. However, the Buddhist culture reached these countries neither uniformly nor at a single time, either in full form or a part thereof and through the traders, merchants and wondering monks.

Perhaps the migration of Buddhism as a religion took place through several movements or processes. The beginning of the process started during the reign of Emperor Ashoka when Buddhism reached Ceylon. However, between the first and seventh century A.D. Buddhism was transmitted to the various regions of South Asia and enjoyed a period of immense creativity and influence.

In the reconstruction of ancient history we have to depend on acceptable materials like archaeological evidences, literary documents in the form of chronicles, epic poems etc. In case of Sri Lanka, fortunately three largely acceptable chronicles are available beside other archaeological materials.

Mahavamsa or *Mahavansa* is one such remarkable chronicle of the Sinhalese kings. It was composed in Pali by the Buddhist scholars and priests under the editorship of a great Buddhist disciple and king Mahanama in fifth century A.D. (Tresidder 1960). This great chronicle covers a wide range of the history of Sinhalese dynasty from Pandukabhaya (377-307 B.C.), Mutasiva (307-247 B.C.), Devanampiya Tissa (247-207 B.C.) and Uttiya (207-197 B.C.) though the chronology of the first two reigns is doubtful (Sastri 1952). Sastri further pointed out "the opening chapter of the *Mahavamsa* contains much edifying legend about the Buddha's visits to the island, the arrival of Vijaya and his encounter with Kuvanna, and his marriage with a princess from the Pandya country"(ibid 1952). In total there are thirty-seven chapters containing the story of the sixty-two kings, for which the chronicle is called the story of the Great Dynasty which ends with the death of king Mahasena in 352 A.D. (Tresidder 1960). Another popular chronicle of Sri Lanka is *Dipavamsa* written only in the fourth century A.D. Some of the scholars of history opined that it is a modified form of *Mahavamsa*. *Kulvamsa* or the Lesser Dynasty was written only after the thirteenth century which contains the story down through the last of the Kandyan rulers, Sri Wickrame Rajasinha who was deposed by the British in 1815 (ibid 1960).

Senaveratna, K.M. De Silva, and other Ceylonese historians have given wonderful information derived from the great Ceylonese chronicle *Mahavamsa* about the spread of Buddhism in Sri Lanka in different times. We come to know from these studies that Buddha himself took the first initiative in the spread of his own thought after attaining enlightenment. This propagation of his thought was not restricted only to his own territory. It also entered other neighbouring countries. Refering to a legend, Senaveratna wrote that Lord Buddha visited Sri Lanka on three distinct occasions after attaining his Buddhahood, in the ninth month, fifth year and eighth year. His second visit was at Nagadipa during the reign of Naga King Mahodora. King Mahodora was in dispute with his nephew on the possession of a gem-setted throne of gold. Buddha amicably settled the dispute with his blessings. The Nagas embraced Buddhism. This time Buddha promised to visit Kelaniya in later occasion, which was fulfilled after three years when Buddha went along with five hundred *bhikhus*. Kelaniya Dagaba stands today to commemorate this occasion. It is also said that Buddha's footprint is still present at Adam's peak in Sri Lanka (Senaveratna 1997, Gupta 1953).

After the consecretion of Devanampiya Tissa as the King of Lanka, he sent an embassy to Magadha. A large delegation headed by the king's nephew Maharittha came to Magadha with costly presents along with five symbols of insignia of royalty – a sword, umbrella, diadem, slipper and fan. The party embarked at Jambukola (Dambakola) for India. After seven days voyage they reached Tamalitti (Tamluk) and then travelled to Pataliputta (Patna), the capital of Magadha. The Sinhalese embassy stayed at Pataliputta for five months (Senaveratna 1997, Gupta 1953).

Ashoka had given a warm welcome to the Sinhalese delegation and being delighted he sent not only the five insignia of royalty as it was customery at that time but also various costly articles along with conch and sacred water of the Ganges. The party returned to Anuradhapura handed over the presents to Devanampiya Tissa along with the message of Ashoka wherein he expressed that Devanampiya Tissa would be consecreted for the second time as a disciple of Lord Buddha (ibid 1997).

Afterwards Mahindra, son of Ashoka (brother in other opinion) came to Lanka with a mission to properly convert the population of Sri Lanka to Buddhism. It may be mentioned that Mahindra came to Lanka along with his nephews Sumana and Bhanduka and four Theras Itthiya, Uttiya, Sambala and Bhaddasala. In honour of the message of his friend Ashoka, king of Lanka embraced the new religion and thereafter Buddhism spread rapidly in Sri Lanka. Buddhism took such a firm base that till today a large number of Sinhalese belong to this faith even after many centuries. A *vihara* or monastery was built on the top of Missaka mountain (present Mihintale) to commemorate the conversion of the king of Lanka. It became a pilgrimage centre of Ceylon where Buddhism has officially established its base (ibid 1997).

During his stay at Lanka, Mahindra felt the need of services of Buddhist nun, accordingly he wrote to Ashoka to send Sanghamitta, daughter of Ashoka, as there was no qualified priestess as such. Mahindra also requested his sister to bring a branch of sacred Bodhi, under which Gautama attained his Buddhahood. Ashoka agreed to sent Sanghamitta and Devanampiya Tissa sent his prime minister, Maharittha to escort princess Sanghamitta. The voyage from Pataliputta started across the Ganges touching Tamalitti and arrived at Jambukola in due course. Interestingly, the voyage of Pataliputta was very big. Sanghamitta came along with eleven nuns. The escorts appointed by Ashoka were eight princes of Magadhian royal blood (Bogut, Sumitta, Sangot, Devgot, Damgot, Hirugot, Sisigot and Jutindhara), eight nobles from the families of ministers, eight persons from the families of Brahmans, eight persons from the families of traders together with a number of representative of clans like Hyaena, the Sparrow-hawk and a few caste people from the weavers, potters and others as well as the Nagas and the Yakkhas.

The sacred Bodhi tree had been brought to Lanka by Sanghamitta in a golden vase and it was planted at Anuradhapura. It grew in eight shoots later on which were planted in various parts of Ceylon. The original Bodhi tree is still present even after many centuries. Devanampiya Tissa founded a royal park Mahamegha near the capital city which became an important centre of Buddhism in Sri Lanka (ibid 1997, Gupta 1953)

Afterwards Devanampiya Tissa expressed his desire to built a stupa or monument in Lanka. Mahindra sent Sumana to his father Ashoka at Pataliputta) to bring some relics of the great sage and accordingly Sumana brought alms-bowl full of relics and handed over to Mahindra. Stupa was built at Missaka mountain which was thenceforth called as Cetiya-Pabbata. Another stupa was built under personal supervision of the king at Maha-Naga-Park where the collar bone relic was rested.

After the death of King Mahasena (334-362 A.D.) his son Meghavarna ascended the throne. Buddha's tooth relic was brought from Kalinga and consecrated in a temple in the ninth year of his reign. (Majumdar 1954). Unlike Devanampiya Tissa, Meghavarana took much initiative for the propagation of Buddhism. We come to learn from a Chinese historian as referred to by Radha Kumud Mukherjee that the king deputed two monks, one of whom was the king's own brother to observe the Buddhist monastery at Buddhagaya and also to pay homage to the lord Buddha. Afterwards Meghavarna sent a formal embassy to Samudragupta with valuable gifts, containing gems and precious articles. The proposal was that the king of Lanka desired to built a *vihara* at Buddhagaya for the Sinhalese pilgrims. The then emperor of Magadha was pleased and granted the permission and Meghavarna built a *vihara* in the name Mahabodhi Sangharama which can accommodate one thousand monks at a time. So it appears that both Sri Lanka and Magadha had maintained some sort of religious as well as political relations in those days.

A good number of wondering monks and scholars went to Sri Lanka for the propagation of Buddhism from time to time. Their contribution on Buddhist literature is of immense importance. During the reign of the Sinhalese king Mahanama (409-31 A.D.), the Indian scholar Buddha Ghosa went to Sri Lanka and stayed there for a considerable period of time. He was basically a brahmin and learnt Vedas but afterwards he became influenced by a Buddhist disciple Revata and became Buddhist monk. *Encyclopedia of Religion* recorded that he went to Ceylon in about 430 A.D. and was a great systematiser of early Buddhist literature. He studied Sinhalese commentaries under Sanghapala at the Mahavira and later on he retranslated this into Pali. His major works were *Samantapasadika, Papancasudani, Saratthappakasini* and the *Manoratha Purani*, on the *Sutta Pitaka*. Beside, he was also the author of Jataka commentary and *Parittahakatha* and other books. He lived in Ganthakara Vihara and after completing his work he returned to Jambudvipa (Saletore 1986).

Another Indian scholar, Buddha Dutta went to Sri Lanka though the exact period of his arrival is not clear. Some historian have the opinion that he was contemporary to Buddha Ghosa and with the advice of the latter he retranslated *Attatkatha*. There were other notable commentators like Dhammapala, Upasena and Mahanama (Encyclopaedia of religion 1987).

Majumdar wrote on the basis of a Chinese account that Vajrabodhi, an Indian monk was invited by a Sinhalese king Sri Sila or Sri Silamegha-Varana (718-719 A.D.). On his way from China to India he halted at Sri Lanka (Majumdar 1954).

In the late medieval period another scholar, Ramchandra Kavi Bharati, went to Sri Lanka and he became a disciple of the great Sinhalese Buddhist poet Bhadanta Rahul. He learnt Tripitaka and published three important Buddhist literature, *Brittaratnakar Panjika, Brittamala* and *Bhaktisatakam*.

Even during the reign of Dutta Gamini, fourteen Theras came from India for the foundation of a mahastupa by the king of Sri Lanka. The name of these Theras is mentioned in the *Dipavamsa*.

In the Ceylonese chronicles, the Pali expression for Tamil is Damila. These chronicles suggest the existence of Pandya kingdom and its capital even at the time of Vijayasima, the great conquerer of Ceylon. There are also references of contact between south India and Ceylon in the writings of Megasthenes and in the different rock-edicts of Emperor Ashoka. Nilkantha Sastri in his book *Age of the Nandas and Mauryas* had explained the long and continuous relations between south India and Tambapani (present Sri Lanka). The *Encyclopaedia of Indian Culture* has given a beautiful description on the Tamil immigration in Sri Lanka, on the basis of the three Ceylonese chronicle and other available writings on these lands. In the *Mahavamsa* a few important names of Damilas have been referred to like Sena, Gutta, or Guttaka, Pulahattha, Vatuka and Niliya. The chronicle further affirms that some of them settled in Ceylon and also gained political control on some of the regions of Ceylon. It is said that these Damilas were brought into this country by the Ceylonese rulers as captives and also as mercenaries. Interestingly, with the passage of time, Damila *bhasa* (language) became popular in Ceylon due to the settlement of Damila population there. As the rulers of Ceylon brought the Damilas as horse traders, hence their apparent visit was from a commercial angle. But the situation changed afterwards. During the reign of Suratissa, the younger brother of Mahatissa, two powerful Damilas, Sena and Guttaka who used to bring horses to Ceylon and were popular as horse traders attacked this island with a great army. As the battle was sudden and unexpected, the Damilas defeated the Ceylonese king Suratissa easily and reigned the island for twenty-two years. However, subsequently they were overpowered by the Ceylonese king Asela. Afterwards in 145 B.C. a Tamil noble Elara came from Tamil country and defeated Asela and ruled for forty-four years. Later on Elara was defeated and killed by a great Ceylonese king Duttagamini. Some interesting events happened thereafter. Duttagamini, after killing Elara, built a monument where the body of the deceased had been cremated and ordained worship there. It is said that Elara was from a noble descent and was noted for his even justice to his friend and foe alike during his tenure at Ceylon. Duttagamini was successful in establishing peace in Ceylon but after his reign, seven Damilas came to Ceylon and fought with the King Lanjakatissa in the battle of Kolambalaka. The king was defeated and Pulahatta, a Damila became king of Ceylon. This time the Damila kings reigned for fourteen years and seven months. Afterwards Vatagamini Abhaya ruled Ceylon for twelve years and three months. Some intersting phenomena happened after this period. A few Damila queens married Sinhalese kings and by then the Damilas had come to stay in Ceylon and played the role of mercenaries to the powerful Sinhalese king.

Large-scale immigration of the Tamils took place in Sri Lanka after the arrival of Sri Vijaya and his companions. It is said that Vijaya himself established good relationship with the nearest Indian king of Madura after conforming his political control on this island country. Perhaps he sent a marriage proposal with the princess of Madura to the king along with huge valuable gems and pearls. The king of Madura was pleased with this proposal and he sent not only his own daughter but also a good number of maidens for Vijaya's companions. The king also sent "craftsman and a thousand families of the eighteen guilds with his daughter" (Senaveratna 1997). The troupe disembarked at Mahalittha (present Mantola). As a result of such relation a considerable number of population emigrated to Ceylon.

With the migration of people from south India to Ceylons, different Hindu religious cults perhaps reached this island country. As Buddhism was already a dominant religion with the patronisation of the Ceylonese kings, Hindu gods and deities were incorporated into Buddhist pantheon and they were given Buddhist recognition. In the early Sinhala iconography there is place for the Hindu gods like Vishnu and Saman (Laksmana) along with their consorts (The Encyclopaedia of Religion 1987 Vol-13).

South Indian influence became strong under the dominance of the Cholas around 1000 A.D. A small Chola temple was built at Polonnaruwa (Sive Devale). Harle mentioned that a large number of Hindu images both made of stone and bronzes were imported from Tamil Nadu and some of these were made by the local carpenters. South Indian deity Tara became popular as Pattini Devi at eastern Sri Lanka in the seventh or eighth century (Harle 1986). In this regard Gananath Obeyesekere wrote that the goddess Pattini is one of the most popular folk deities among the Buddhists and the Hindus of Sri Lanka. The deity has been worshipped in Sri Lanka and south India for fifteen hundred years or so. Her life is also the theme of one of the greatest poems in Tamil literature, the Cilappatikaram, probably composed during the period 500-800 A.D. The cult has died out in south India or has been assimilated into the Kali or other mother goddess cults of India (Obeysekere 1984, Gupta 1953).

The above discussion on the spread of Buddhism in Sri Lanka reveals that Buddhism had made a bridge between India and Sri Lanka. The royal embassy sent by the king of Sri Lanka, Devanampiya Tissa, indicates that Sri Lanka had some early experience of Buddhism either through Buddha himself when he visited Sri Lanka or through the traders and the immigrants. It might so happen that some of the followers of Sri Vijaya, the first king of Sri Lanka, were Buddhist and through them Buddhism founded its base in this island of Sri Lankan, though the religion did not flourish at a broad scale. Offering of presentations suggest that the interactions of the kings of Sri Lanka and India were cordial and honourable. The prolonged stay of a high profile group of Sri Lankan at Pataliputra denotes that they might have studied the philosophy of Buddhism and acquired experience about the practicality of this religion. Ashoka's return of gifts and acknowledgement of second time coronation of Devanampiya Tissa as king of Sri Lanka clearly indicates that both the countries had established both political as well as religious relationship through cordial understanding among them. This is reflected in the consequent phases when Ashoka's son

Mahindra along with his close kin went to Sri Lanka for the spread of Buddhism at a large and wide scale. Further the voyage of Sanghamitta along with huge co-followers of different sections of society especially the higher officials on the one hand and the artisans on the other indicates that at least India was some how advanced in technological progress. Perhaps weaving, pottery and other handicrafts either were not available in Sri Lanka or were in a crude form. And most probably introduction of weaving and pottery might have started only in this period in Sri Lanka. Buddhist arts and crafts also reached Sri Lanka through these artisans of India.

After the establishment of Buddhism in Sri Lanka in full form, Sri Lanka also took the responsibility of its spread. In the third or second century B.C. the monks of Sri Lanka established Sinhala *vihara* at Nagarjunikonda in Andhra Pradesh. It is to be noted here that perhaps Buddhism did not flourish in south India at par with other parts of India.

In course of time the relationship developed at the educational level. Different scholars were invited to Sri Lanka for transcription of Buddhist canon. Buddha Ghosa and other Indian scholars reached Sri Lanka and lived there for a long time during the rule of Mahanama (409 to 431 A.D.). Even in the late medieval period Ram Chandra Kabi Bharati, a Buddhist scholar of Bengal went to Sri Lanka and became a disciple of great Sinhalese poet Bhadanta Rahul. The period of his arrival at Sri Lanka is said to be within 1245 to 1467 A.D. (Choudhury 1995).

Hinduism reached the island of Sri Lanka through the Chola and Damila kings who settled there in different periods from the time of Vijaya to the late medieval period and was blended with Buddhist culture and religion that already existed in the island country of Sri Lanka.

Maldives

The Republic of Maldives consists of about 1009 tiny islands stretching down 764 km of the Indian Ocean. The chain of islands form a garland, hence it is popular as 'Maladive.' The people call themselves Divehi, meaning islander. It's geographical location in the Indian Ocean made it accessible to the traders from many parts of South Asia and led to considerable cultural influences there on. All these contacts enriched the cultural heritage of Maldives and made their culture complex too. Unfortunately the cultural heritage of Maldives has rarely been described because these islands have been virtually ignored by the travellers and scholars for some reasons. Maldives was visited mainly by the seafarers as the history suggest. Shipwrecking was very common phenomena all those days because of dangerous underwater walls of coral reefs.

There are very limited sources to understand the history and culture of Maldives. The earliest account on these islands is available from Francois Pyrard, a Frenchman who suffered shipwreck there in 1602 and was forced to stay there for five and half years. His writing was almost like an ethnographic account. In 1830, two Englishmen Yong and Christopher were deputed to Maldives as a part of marine survey team in the interest of the Britishers of India. They recorded some information on these islands. The most significant contribution on Maldives is of H.C.P. Bell. He was deputed by the Government of Ceylon to study Maldivian Buddhist antiquities. Basically he was an archaeologist and had long experience on the history and archaeology of Ceylon. His wonderful book on Maldives has a wealth of data on language, Buddhist remnants, and Sinhala affinities. Numerous articles were also published by Bell which are useful in understanding the history and culture of Divehi people. Clarence Maloney also wrote a book on the people of Maldives which gives us enormous information on this island country, especially on the cultural history.

The present Divehi people are the followers of Islam. The people of this country became Islamised only in 1153 A.D. and the history of these islands is available only from this period. The previous references are sporadic and to some extent conjectural. A recent publication of an Encyclopaedia on the SAARC mentioned in the preface of its Maldives volume "there was Dravidian population from south India as early as the fourth century B.C. Aryans from India and Ceylon came later to dominate these islands. Buddhism was widely practised until 1153 A.D." (Encyclopaedia of SAARC, Maldives 1997). Reynolds also expressed "it is undisputed that the islanders were Buddhist before they adopted Islam" (Reynolds 1978). It is also evident from a folk tale collected by Bell and referred to by Maloney that Kalaminja, the son of king Koimala reigned as a Buddhist for twelve years and was then converted to Islamic faith in the early twelfth century (Maloney 1980). Due to lack of archaeological work in these islands, we do not have any direct evidence of the antiquity of Buddhism. However, H.C.P. Bell's study on Maldives clearly indicates that Buddhism had become the state religion of Maldives and stupas had been built in many parts of this country before the twelfth century. Bell observed the existence of stupas in more than ten islands ranging from south to north central region (Maloney 1980). The most important archaeological remains of Buddhism like a stupa and also a Bodhi tree were found in southern part of the country at Gan, in Seenu atoll. Unfortunately these remains were destroyed during the foundation of an airstrip by the British. Another interesting information noted by Maloney is that in Male there is no remains of stupa but Buddhist artifacts as well as a stone head of Buddha were found during the construction of a house. It is also said that there was a large Bodhi tree near the present palace of the President (Maloney 1980). Maloney further wrote that even some early travellers like Gardiner, also noted the existence of the stupas in Maldives when he visited these islands in 1900. There was a small museum in the old palace containing a number of Buddhist artifacts including a head of Buddha, a few relic caskets, trinkets and a few silver punch-marked coins.

In 1940s Maldivian Government conducted an expedition and found a stone head of Buddha in the island of Toddu. The party also observed existence of seven stupas in this island. Beside this, round coins in a plate, a few long silver coins and other relics in caskets were also found in Buddhist stupas elsewhere (Maloney 1980).

Maloney expressed that though Bell could not give the real chronology of the pre-Muslim period of Maldives in absence of relevant archaeological findings, "there is evidence from Bell's antiquarian investigations that Buddhist civilisation achieved its apex there from the ninth to the twelfth centuries" (Maloney 1980).

Dr. Paranavitana, an archaeologist of Sri Lanka examined the photographs of some of these stupas. He also observed "the relic caskets found in the Maldivian stupas are almost identical in shape with similar caskets found at ancient stupas in Ceylon" (cf Maloney 1980). It will be worth mentioning that the ethos of Buddhism in Sri Lanka was established between the second century B.C. to the fourth century B.C. (Maloney 1980).

Two important inscriptions were also found in south India, which refer to the relationship between India and Maldives. The first one is Vayalur pillar inscriptions of the Pallava king Rajasimha II and "the second inscription pertaining to Maldives is of the time of the Chola king Rajaraja (985-1014 A.D.) who founded the revived Chola empire" (Maloney 1980). Medieval history of Deccan also suggests that the Pandyas conquered both Ceylon and Maldives (Sinha 1964).

The evidences of Buddhist stupas and other Buddhist remnants found in different atolls of Maldives islands clearly indicate that the Buddhist tradition had existed for a considerable period before Islamisation. Reynolds wrote that the classical language of this country was Sanskrit and the scripts they used were derived from Brahmi. After conversion to Islam, both these features changed (Reynolds 1978). Here a question naturally arises as to how and by whom Buddhism reached this island country ? The answer of this question is difficult as the chronological history of this country is obscure due to lack of serious archaeological research in Maldives. Though an attempt had been made by the government of Sri Lanka sending a renowned scholar H.C.P. Bell in early twenties but unfortunately he failed to do it because of high water level and coral sand of these islands. However, it is apparent from whatever information he collected on Buddhist antiquity that Buddhism was brought from Sri Lanka to Maldives. Sri Lankan archaeologists also found the resemblance of relic caskets between Ceylon and Maldives. The mythical stories noted by Bell also indicate the possibility of cultural affinities of the Divehi people with the people of Ceylon. Though another version of the same story heard by Maloney in other part of Maldives tempt us to think about the link between India and Maldives. Hence, the chances of Indian cultural affinity with Divehi people are difficult to ignore. But one can ascertain that the principal cultural affinities of the Maldivians are with the Sinhalese.

Another dimension of religious linkage has been shown by Maloney on the basis of three Jataka tales referring to Maldives. He suggested that the Gujaratis actually settled there in pre-Buddhist time. The other Jataka tales suggest that ships from Gujarat going to South-East Asia stopped at Maldives in search of treasures (Maloney 1980). Some of the words in Divehi language indicate the names of Hindu deities like Candu, Chamundi and Skanda. The astrological system of Maldives is clearly of north Indian origin, but we cannot ascertain whether it came to these islands from pre-Buddhist Sri Lanka or directly from north India. Festival like kite flying, celebrated on a particular day in Maldives resemble with the *Patang Utri Dibas* in Gujarat. The name of the sacred plant *tulsi* of the Hindus is also found in Divehi language as *tulusudo*. The above information indicates that there was early connection between the Gujaratis and the Divehis and Hindu religion reached to Maldives through western India. Maloney expressed his views in this regard that the roots of Sinhalese and Divehi culture and language are traceable to western India i.e. Gujarat and Punjab. The pre-Buddhist north-west Indian civilisation was transplanted to Sri Lanka and later extended through sea to other coast of South-East Asia (Maloney 1980).

Bhutan

The Himalayan kingdom of Bhutan has a deep rooted history but the early history as well as the knowledge about the original inhabitants is still obscure. The valuable manuscripts and early documents of this country were destroyed due to fire at Sonagachi in 1828 and at Poonakha in 1832. Further the earthquake of 1896 completed the destruction in this regard (Singh 1972). However, some sort of incomplete record could be gathered from the legends, myths and a few manuscripts found in other's possession. G.N. Mehra believed that neither the Drukpas were the original inhabitants of this country nor Bhutan as a geographical entity existed during the larger part of the first millennium (Mehra 1974). According to a legend of the seventh century B.C. Sangaldip from Kooch (present Koch Behar) in Assam subdued Bengal and Bihar and extended his sway to Bhutan. Thereafter

Bhutan was under the Indian rulers till several centuries. Both Bhutanese and Indian tradition accept that Bhutan was ruled by the Indian chiefs under the tutelage of Kamrupa upto 650 A.D. It was separated from Kamrupa only after the death of Bhaskaravarman. After this, any king was able to hold his authority on this country which resulted to the Tibetan incursion in Bhutan around 861-900 A.D. (Singh 1972). Under such a situation, Bhutan was deeply influenced by Indian culture and tradition. There was "close similarity of ancient rituals, frescoes and musical instruments of Bhutan with those of ancient Hindu kingdoms" (Mehra 1974).

The available early history of Bhutan is very much linked with religion especially Buddhism. Mehra and some other scholars believe that Bhuddhism came to Bhutan from Tibet at the first instance, as the Bhutanese people mostly follow Tibetan Buddhism. They try to trace the history of religion of Bhutan from Tibetan sources. However, B. Chakravarti, believed that Bhutan was closer to the Surya Pahar (Goalpara of Assam) and the Bhutanese had greater contact with the Buddhist universities like Nalanda and Vikramsila than Tibet. He further pointed out that there was regular communication through Bengal and Assam duars for trade and other purposes. Some cattle herders, traders, travellers and medicants of Bhutan came in contact with the people of Buddhist sect living in Assam and Bengal earlier than Tibetans. In support of his statement he cited the inscriptions on stone at Buddha Vaksita and the votive stupas found at Goalpara (Chakravarti 1979).

Buddhism of the Tibetan form became the state religion of Bhutan as early as the eighth or ninth century A.D. The noted Indian saint and teacher of Nalanda University, Guru Padmasambhava, the real founder of Tibetan Buddhism visited Bhutan twice. A legendary figure, Sindhu Raja, an Indian king who is believed to be reigning at Bumthang, invited the great Guru. The legend further suggests that

Sindhu Raja lost his eldest son in a war with Raja Nabudara of Indian plains and plunged into grief. He called on Padmasambhava who was in Tibet at that time for the propagation of Buddhism. The great Guru provided solace to the king and saved his life. Sindhu Raja was convinced with the efficacy of the Buddhist faith. Interestingly, the rival king Nabudara also became a Buddhist. Thus the seed of Buddhism was sown in the soil of Bhutan. (Singh 1972, Mehra 1974, Chakravarti 1980). There was a mutual contact between the two kings in the presence of Guru Padmasambhava. A boundary pillar was also erected between the two kingdoms at Nalong in Khen area. Temples and monasteries were erected in honour to commemorate the visit of the great saint. Scroll paintings or *thankas* were installed and worshipped. The biography of Sindhu Raja or the *Sindhuraja-i-Namthar* indicates that many Indians came and settled down in Bumthang and Punakha during this period (Chakravarti 1980).

According to a legend, the large-scale Tibetan immigration took place in Bhutan in early part of the ninth century to drive out the invaders of India. Later on these Tibetans liked this country and refused to go back. A large-scale influx of Tantrik Lamas took place during the twelfth to fourteenth century in western Bhutan (Mehra 1974, Chakravarti 1980). Buddhism in its Tibetan form established its strong foot hold in no time.

Bhutan was divided into a number of small principalities, having a political or religious head. Buddhism was gradually gaining ground in different sections, of the society. The Khens of central Bhutan were organised and powerful but were not yet Buddhist by religion.

Niladhwaja, a Khen chief, with the help of an influential Brahmin overpowered the Pala dynasty of Bengal and established Khen dynasty, at least for three generations. The last king of this dynasty Nilambara, was overthrown by Hussain Shah in 1498 A.D. It is said that the Brahmin became the chief minister of Raja Niladhwaja and brought many Brahmins from Mithila (Chakravarti 1980). S.K. Chatterjee observed:

> Niladhwaja is said to have actively worked for the Hinduisation of his people although he fought and overthrew the last section of the Pala family of Bengal. The Khens claim to be Kayasthas, but it would appear they are Indo-Mongoloid in their affinity.
> (cf Chakravarti 1980).

An Assamese chronicle, *Darrang Rajbansabali* of the Darrang kings recorded that Narashingha, son of Koch king Bisva Singha, fled to Bhutan and established a kingdom there. The dynasty was popular as Dharmarajas with capital at Punakha.

There was glorious achievements by the Bhutanese people during the early period. *Rajatarangini*, the Sanskrit chronicle of the Kashmiri kings reveals that a learned Bhutanese scholar named Stonpa became the preceptor of the king of Kamrupa and he was entrusted to escort the princes Amrtaprabha. Stonpa himself built a stupa there in the early fifth century A.D. (Chakravarti 1980).

The above discussion on Bhutan indicates that the early rulers of Bhutan came from the Indian plains. Automatically the ancient Indian civilisation spread to this region and dominated political, social as well as the religious life of the people. Buddhism reached Bhutan at least from two sources, from India on the one hand and Tibet on the other. Today the Bhutanese follow mainly Buddhism in its Tibetan form. Buddhism had moulded the Bhutanese civilisation and developed the national outlook, attitudes and aspirations. It was possible only through mutual understanding and co-operation between India and Bhutan.

Nepal

Two major religious groups, namely, the Hindus and the Buddhists have lived in harmony and tranquility for centuries in the Himalayan kingdom of Nepal. How and when these religions came to this land is an interesting question. Geographically and economically Nepal was inseparable from the Indo-gangetic plains of India. Buddhism entered this valley long before the Christian era. Interestingly, all the ruling dynasties of this Himalayan kingdom, the Lichchavis, the Thakuris, the Karnatakas, the Mallas and lastly the Shahs migrated from the plains. Though the early history of Nepal is full of conjectural information and her chronological history is obscure, it is generally accepted that historically some parts of the valley is as old as the very oldest part of India. Earliest inhabitants of Nepal were animists. Buddhist religion and aesthetic taste were imposed upon animism. Varma opined that the religious life of the Nepalese was influenced by the main streams of Buddhism and Brahmanism of the Indian plains, supported by the succesive waves of immigration from India (Varma 1972). He further wrote on the basis of archaeological evidences that Brahmanism came to Nepal during the Gupta-Vakataka period and during the reign of Ksrnata-Khatriya dynasty of Ganges–Yamuna valley and also from Deccan (ibid 1972).

If we look at the population structure of this country, it appears that the earliest inhabitants were probably members of Kirata tribe of Indo-Mongolian stock with Tibeto-Burman tongue. These people probably came from Assam and northeast India. (Pemble 1971). They came in masses; as artisans, traders, professionals, peasants and merged with local population and in course of time emerged as ruling aristocrats (Subba & Chettri 1998). In early part of civilisation, Buddhism was probably the main religion of Nepal, but when the system of monarchy replaced the old tribal government, the kings were mostly Hindus. These kings modeled themselves on the style and activities of the monarchs of the plains. The Kiratas were apparently displaced by the Lichchavis of north Indian origin. They founded the first Hindu dynasty in Nepal and adopted the titles used by the Rajputs. These Lichchavi kings introduced the classical Hindu varna system in Nepal (Pemble 1971). They ruled this country from the first until eighth century, built a powerful empire and extended their suzerainty. A Lichchavi princess was married to Chandragupta I at the beginning of the fourth century A.D. and the Lichchavis became powerful due to this relation with Gupta empire (Majumdar et al. 1963). In 704 A.D. or thereafter the Lichchavi dynasty came to an end. It is interesting to note that Ansuvarman, a noble descent of Thakur family got married to the daughter of a Lichchavi king Shivadeva and became a defacto ruler of the country (Thapa 1981). The Thakuri dynasty ruled Nepal for about two hundred years and at the end of the eleventh century under the king Sankara Deva, the valley reverted to anarchy. The Mallas took the position. The period was very disturbed and uncertain due to raids from north India and from the Karnata king of Tirhut. Hari Simha of Tirhut made his way into the valley of Nepal. He was a great patroniser of Sanskrit. He exercised a strong influence on the development of Hinduism in the valley. During the reign of Jaya Sthithi Malla, a notable ruler of Nepal, it became a sanctuary for the laws and tradition of Hinduism. The laws of Hinduism were recorded and codified by the Pundits of India.

Spread of Buddhism in Nepal
Lord Buddha himself, after attaining enlightenment made a pilgrimage to Nepal, accompanied by one thousand three

hundred and fifty *bhikhus* (medicant ascetics). Satiputta, Maudgalyana, Ananda were the main followers of Buddha during the latter's visit to Nepal, along with the Raja of Benaras including his large courtiers. During the great master's visit, Kirati king Jitedasti (about 450 B.C.) sowed the seed of his teachings among the people of this valley. Several of his followers were deputed for the spread of this new religion (Brown 1989). In the third century B.C. Mauryan emperor Ashoka, after proclaiming Buddhism as state religion in his dynasty, became active in the spread of this religion. He further introduced and also patronised Buddhism in Nepal. Ashoka travelled from his capital Pataliputra to various Buddhist holy places in the valley (ibid 1989). Probably Buddhism was basically a sectarian religion until the visit of Ashoka. Ashoka's pilgrimage to the birth place of Buddha is clearly inscribed in the pillar of Rummindei (Lumbini) and Nigali Sagar. Nepalese tradition further affirms that the pilgrimage of Ashoka under the guidance of Upagupta was continued into Nepal. He founded the city of Patan which is popular as Ashoka Patan or Lalit Patan. The Nepalese chronicle, *Swambhupuran* also recorded the description of Ashoka's journey to Nepal. This has been referred to by Rahul Sankrityayan. Ashoka built six *chaityas* or stupas and one *vihara* at Deo-Patan. Further he also permitted his daughter to marry a Buddhist devotee at Deo-Patan (Landon 1976, Brown 1989).

With the introduction of Hinduism in the valley by the monarchial rulers of plains, Buddhism took a somewhat different course. However, during the period of Pala dynasty in Bengal (eighth century A.D.) Vajrayana and other tantric affiliation came to occupy an important position in the religious life of the people of eastern India. Acharya Shantarakshit (626 A.D.), Guru Padmasambhava (700 A.D.) and lastly Atisa Dipankara (1052 A.D.) introduced tantric cult in the Mahayana form of Buddhism. The magical doctrines and religious practices played a great role not only in Buddhism in Nepal but also in her existing Brahmanism too (Varma 1972). Almost every temple and religious establishment in Nepal adopted the mode of worship which basically is a form of Indian Tantrism. Professor Radha Kamal Mukherjee wrote in his book *The Culture and Art of India* that in the middle of the eleventh century, Atisa Srijana Dipankara visited Nepal accompanied by Vinayadhara Gyatson, Bhumi Garbha and a prince disciple Bhumi Sangha from western India. Silabhadra and Abhaykara Gupta were also the distinguished co-followers of Atisa (Mukherjee 1984). Another Indian scholar Dinesh Chandra Sen in his famous book in Bengali *Brihat Banga* mentioned that on his way to Tibet via Nepal, Atisa was given a special welcome by the king of Nepal, Raja Ananta Kirti. The king also offered an elephant for carrying ritual articles. To commemorate the occasion of the great master's visit the king of Nepal made a *Than Vihar*. The most significant point of this occasion was that the Raja allowed his son Padmaprava to get converted into Buddhism. His son became a disciple of Dipankara and renamed as Devendra according to Buddhist custom.

Mukherjee is of the opinion that there was regular interaction between the monasteries of Nalanda, Vikramsila, Jagaddla and Odantapuri of India and Tibet as well as Nepal. This relationship was intimate and fruitful which continued for many centuries. Mahayana, Vajrayana, Sahaja and Tantrism left considerable impression on religion and culture of these countries (Mukherjee 1984).

Another striking feature of religious conjecture took place during Muslim invasion in eastern India and consequent attack on the famous Buddhist monasteries located at Nalanda and Vikramsila. Under such a situation hundreds of Buddhist monks seem to have fled to Nepal. This flight of Buddhist talents were honoured and accepted by the royal house of Nepal. Similarly a large section of the Hindus left the Indo-Gangetic plains of India and went to western hills of Nepal for a peaceful sanctuary during the twelfth century. The Rajputs came to Nepal accompanying their brahmin priests as spiritual advisors (Subba 1989). Importantly, these Rajputs were later known as Thakurs or Thakuris of the great kshatriya rulers of Nepal.

Nepal is an example of peaceful co-existence of two religions, Buddhism and Hinduism. Many of the kings of Nepal claim themselves to belong to the solar dynasty of India. Many places of Nepal were named after the pilgrimages of India like Kaski in western Nepal against Kasi of India. A hillock near Pashupatinath temple is called Kailash. One interesting phenomenon is available here. King Pratapa Malla constructed a tank in honour of his beloved queen which was filled up with the sanctified water of sacred pilgrimages of India, as the inscription recorded. The four faces of Pashupatinath is said to correspond to the (four important *tirthas* of India) *Char-dham* namely Badrinath, Rameswaram, Dwarka and Jagannath (Varma 1972).

The spread of religion was a unique cultural movement that brought and maintained the unity of South Asian civilisation for many centuries in the past. Both Hinduism and Buddhism existed in Nepal with tolerance and co-operation between each others' religion. Buddhist art and architectural designs are available in both Buddhist monasteries as well as in Hindu temples. A good number of Buddhist refugees and scholars from India and Tibet propagated Buddhism and wrote religious scriptures during their stay in Nepal. In the medieval period some Malla kings of Nepal married Indian princesses of Vaishali, Mithila, Magadha, Rajasthan, Bengal, Assam and Tripura. Another important incident, recorded by the historions, was that a

Nepali king had conquered the king of Kashmir. (Subba and Chettri 1998).

Through Myths, Epics and Chronicles

Study of myth remained a fascinating area for the cultural anthropologists as well as scholars of other disciplines too. The word myth originated from the Greek word 'mythos', meaning 'saying' or 'story'. The term 'mythology' usually refers to the corpus of myths associated with a particular cultural tradition. Myths are the stories that the human imagination construct around the 'animated' natural objects. However, anthropologist like Franz Boas believe that it would be possible to reconstruct the nature of traditional societies of the past from myths, hence it is an essential part of ethnographic investigation. Folklorists believe that they can identify the society in which the myth originated and they can also reconstruct the original version of the myth. The similarities and pattern of the myths available in different regions indicate cultural linkage in the distant past.

The knowledge of myth comes mainly from secondary sources like diaries of travellers, missionaries and colonial administrators. These mythical or folk stories generally travel easily from one group of people to another and hence there is enough scope of change in the process. It is difficult to ascertain the origin of the myth. However, myth sometimes associated with ancient history, helps in the depiction of a particular civilisation, as writing and inscriptions sometimes witness to their mythological heritage.

Myth and folk tale, the two modes of narrative, have much in common. These exist in multiple versions. According to Willis, "one can say that folktales are domesticated myths," stories put together from mythic elements with the dual purpose of entertaining and pointing some moral about human society (Willis 1993).

South Asia is one of the most culturally diverse regions of the world. Mythical stories associated with the people of South Asia reflect many facets of cultural heritage of this region. Both Hinduism and Buddhism disseminated throughout the region since ancient times. In spite of these religious diversities, certain ideas give South Asian mythology a unique character of its own.

From the very beginning of Indian culture there has been a continuous interaction between the different religious, linguistic and social groups which have resulted in emergence of rich mythological heritage. Epics in the forms of *Puranas*, *Ramayana* and *Mahabharata* are the great storehouse of religious and mythical traditions.

All these mythical texts are the only sources providing a glimpse of the social and historical picture of the past. These also give us the idea of relationship between the nations as well as people of the past. Though the historical acceptance of these facts is debatable but still these bear a good deal of reliability too, which cannot be ignored easily.

Sri Lanka

The existence of relationship between India and Sri Lanka has been mentioned even in the days of Puranas. It is apparent from the *Skandapurana* that first incursion of the Aryan Hindus into Sri Lanka occurred under Skanda or Kartikeya, the son of Lrd Shiva for subjugation of Tarakasura. This legend signifies the presence of the Aryans and the spread of worship of Shiva and Kartikeya in Sri Lanka. There is a forest shrine in the south-eastern corner of Sri Lanka called Kartikeya-grama or Katargrama. Even today both the Hindus and Muslims visit the forest shrine as mark of devotion. It is said that Ravana, the king of Sri Lanka was the worshipper of Shiva. This has been mentioned in the verses of *Skandapurana*, chapter-XXI, verses 219-221 (cf De 1976).

The next Aryan invasion was undertaken by Rama and Lakshmana of the Solar dynasty. The legendary history of these heroes has been depicted in the great Sanskrit epic, the *Ramayana*. This long poem, thought to have been written by the great Indian poet Valmiki, describes the conquest of Sri Lanka by Rama, the incarnation of Lord Vishnu, a deity of Hindu Pantheon.

The *Ramayana* is based on the story of Rama, the eldest son of Dasaratha, a prince of the Ikshvaku family of Ayodhya in the Fyzabad district of Oudh. Rama married Sita, the daughter of Janaka, king of Videha in north Bihar. Owing to a palace intrigue, the Ikshvaku prince had to leave his home and go into exile for a period of fourteen years. He moved to the Dandaka forest in the Deccan with his wife and faithful half-brother Lakshmana. He dwelt for sometime on the banks of the Godavari in Panchvati, which is usually identified with present day Nasik in Maharashtra. He came into conflict here with the *Rakshasas* or cannibal chieftains, who were source of disturbance to the peaceful hermits of the locality. Among the hostile chieftains some persons were closely related to Ravana, the mighty king of Sri Lanka. To take avenge, Ravana carried off Sita, wife of Rama to his island home. In their distress Rama allied with Sugriva, Hanumana and other monkey chiefs of Kishkindha and crossed over to Sri Lanka, building a bridge across the Palk Strait. Rama finally killed Ravana and rescued Sita and brought her back to India. Both Rama and Sita are worshipped today by devouted Hindus along with the popular monkey god Hanumana in Sri Lanka. The place, Sitawaka (now called Avisawella) thirty-six miles east of Colombo, commemorate the prison fortress of Sita. Her name is a popular first name of both Sinhalese and Tamil girls of Sri Lanka. The name of Sita is also associated with different natural objects like Sitaela (Sita's stream), Sita-Koonda (Sita's pond), Sitatalawa (Sita's plain). Sitangula is supposed to be the pond where Sita used to bathe (cf De 1976).

It is difficult to say if there is any kernel of historical truth underneath this tale of a prince's adventure in the land of cannibals and monkeys. Rama and Sita are names in the vedic literature, though not always as appellations of human beings. They are, however, in no way connected in the vedic text with the illustrious line of Ikshvakus or the Videhas. The name Ravana is absolutely unknown to Brahmanical or non-Brahmanical literature till we come to the epic themselves or to works like the Kautiliya's *Arthasashtra*, which shows acquaintance with the epics. It is, however, possible that Ikshvaku prince played a leading role in the colonisation of the far south of India, as names of Ikshvaku kings figure prominently in the early inscription of southern India.

An archaeological approach to unveil the story of *Ramayana* has been given by the renowned archaeologist H.D. Sankalia. He expressed that the existence of Ayodhya, Kausambi, Mithila, Kanyakubja and other cities were true at least by 1000 B.C. The core of *Ramayana*, the characters and the story were also true. But Ravana very probably belonged to the Gond tribe and a dark-skinned man of the Chota Nagpur plateau in east, Madhya Pradesh and most probably near Jabbalpur. The Vanaras were the aboriginal tribes of that time. He expressed that the entire episode took place in a compact geographical area. He further noted that the area around Rameshwaram is flat with low sandy mounds. No piece of stone can be found and even the trees are rare with which Rama and his Vanara bands could have built a causeway to Sri Lanka (Sankalia 1973).

The *Ramayana*, the *Mahabharata* and the *Puranas* are not considered as history. But, we cannot ignore all those incidents available in these texts, which appear to be historical. We can ignore all the religious performances and poetic versions, however, these give some indication of the period of such happenings which are also supplemented by other cross references of folk tradition.

The three chronicles of Sri Lanka – the *Mahavamsa*, the *Dipavamsa* and the *Kulavamsa*, which are not epics like the *Ramayana* and the *Mahabharata*, may be considered as the earliest source of information of ancient history of Sri Lanka. The *Dipavamsa* was written in Pali before the *Mahavamsa*. Some scholars opine that a modified form of the *Dipavamsa* is the *Mahavamsa* which was also written in Pali later on. However, the *Mahavamsa* is a much popular chronicle of Sri Lanka's ancient historical deed. The story of Vijaya is available in both the chronicles in some modified form. Rapson wrote "Pali, the literary form of some Indian Prakrit which was transplanted to Ceylon, probably in the third century B.C. became the sacred language of the particular phase of Buddhism which found a permanent home in the island" (Rapson 1960).

Both the chronicles, the *Mahavamsa* and the *Dipavamsa* tell a singular story that a daughter of a king of Vanga (Bengal) and a princess of Kalinga (Orissa) were carried away by a lion who begot a son, Sihabahu (lion arm) and a daughter, Sihasivali. Sihabahu reigned at Sihapura, Lion's town in Lala (Lata in Gujarat). His son Vijaya was banished for his lawlessness and departed from Sihapura. He continued his voyage to Sri Lanka via Supparaka (the modern Sopara, in the Thane district, Maharashtra). At the time of Vijaya's arrival the island was in the possession of the Yakshas, a kind of demi-god. Kuvanna or Kuveni became the consort of Vijaya and he became the king, thereby removing all the Yakshas. The children of this union became the ancestors of the Pulinda tribes (Rapson 1955).

There is another myth regarding Vijaya. De is of the opinion that after the period of *Ramayana* next came the

Manuraja vamsa in Sri Lanka. The kingdom was established by a prince from India. There lived a king Simhabahu and his queen Simasiva at Simhapura in India. They had a son Vijaya. Prince Vijaya and his seven hundred companions were charged for some serious crime and they boarded a ship to leave the country. After a long voyage across the sea they landed in Sri Lanka (543 B.C.). It is generally agreed that the prince of Bengal, Vijaya arrived in the island of Sri Lanka almost at the time of *Nirvana* of Lord Buddha. It is said that Sri Lanka was then occupied by the Yakshas. The prince married a Yaksha princess Kuveni and through her aid he destroyed the kingdom of Yakshas and became the first king of Sri Lanka of the Manuraja vamsa. The Yaksha power disappeared from the island since then. Later Kuveni and her children were discarded by Vijaya and he re-established linkages with India and formed an alliance with Pandya, king of Madura in south India, whose daughter he married. It is said that a good number of probable bride came from Madura along with the princess in exchange of huge pearls, corals and other gifts.

There is difference of opinion with regard to how and when Vijaya arrived at Sri Lanka. But it is generally agreed that Vijaya or Wijaya had been banished for misconduct from the kingdom of Sihapura in Northern India by Sihabahu, Vijaya's father. It has been mentioned by a good number of scholars (De Silva 1981, Hulugalle 1946, De 1976). Hulugalle opines that the first Aryan settlers arrived in Sri Lanka about 500 B.C. and "Vijaya a noble lineage in Vanga(Bengal) but it is probable that he set sail from a port near Broach in the province of Bombay" (Hulugalle 1946). He further mentioned that there was a second stream of immigration from the Ganges valley which formed the substratum of the Aryan population of Ceylon. Name of Ceylon was originally Lanka and it was renamed Simhala after its conquest by Vijaya Simha of Bengal about 543 B.C. (De 1976).

Vijaya was consecrated as king of new Sinhalese dynasty with an early admixture of Tamil blood. Vijaya ruled over Lanka as lord for thirty eight years (Tresidder 1960).

Literature gives us enormous information directly or indirectly of a specific culture in particular time span. The stories, novels, poems enrich the literary tradition, sometimes in the form of long narration or an incident. Some stories are simply myths but there are substratum of historical facts within. The verses of *Chandimangal Kavya*, the earliest known complete narrative of Chandi story composed by Kavi Mukundaram Chakraborty around the end of the sixteenth century narrates linkages between Indian traders and people of Sri Lanka (Sanyal 1982).

The story narates that Dhanapati Saudagar, a rich merchant of Ujani, who was also a devout of Lord Shiva, went to Sri Lanka for trade, in the need of royal estate. On his way to Ceylon he lost all the six ships which sank into the deep sea due to natural calamity (It is said that the incident happened due to displeasure of Devi Chandi). However, he narrowly survived with a solitary ship and reached Sri Lanka. In the confluence of sea near Sri Lanka Dhanapati saw a very unnatural scene, which he expressed to the king of Sri Lanka. Unfortunately, he failed to prove his experience in the court of Sri Lanka and got imprisoned there. After a long period of time, his son Sripati went to Sri Lanka for trade and also in search of his father Dhanapati with seven ships. He was a worshipper of Devi Chandi, so his journey was more or less smooth by the grace of Devi. However, he also observed the same unnatural scene at the confluence of the sea which his father had seen and accordingly he expressed the fact in the court of the king of Sri Lanka. The then king of Sri Lanka, Salibahan became so displeased that he ordered death sentence to Sripati. But by the grace of goddess Chandi he could overcome the problem. He freed himself and his father

Dhanapati and married Sushila, the princess of Sri Lanka and returned to India.

The above story clearly indicates that there was a continuous relation with Sri Lanka and India at least in the sea route. The trade relationship is clearly discernible through this folk story.

Maldives

The ancient history of Maldives is obscure. It is difficult to say when the Divehi people first settled down in these islands nation. The earliest French scholar Francois Pyrad who worked in early 1600 A.D. mentioned that the people of the Maldives began to live in these islands only four hundred years ago. Hence the Divehi's arrival dates back only to 1200 A.D. Interestingly, this period coincides with the popular Koimala myth to the extent of the predecessor of the King Kalaminja. The culture and history of Maldives have rarely been described by travellers, journalists or any other person. In 1920-1922 H.C.P. Bell, an archaeologist, visited the islands to study the Buddhist antiquities in Maldives. He intended to see the culture of the pre-Muslim period of Maldives. Not much excavation could be conducted because of the coral sand soil and the high water level. However, Bell collected a good number of folk tales from the different atolls and also gathered description of the Buddhist stupas available at that time. His account is the most valuable publication on Maldives till today. These folk tales are the only sources to reconstruct the early cultural history of Maldives.

The Koimala story is one of the most important myths of Maldives which is related to the origin of the people. Bell and Maloney have recorded at least five different versions of the same story from different atolls. We would like to analyse the stories of Maldives, which are the earliest sources of reference, to understand the cultural linkages between India and Maldives since the stories bear considerable historical significance.

Koimala myth as recorded by Bell in 1922 : Once upon a time when Maldives was sparsely populated, a prince of royal birth named Koimala, who got married to the princess of Sri Lanka, made a voyage in two vessels from Serendib(Sri Lanka). After reaching Maldives, they rested at the island of Rasgetimu in north Malosmadulul. The people of Maldives proclaimed Koimala as their king. Subsequently Koimala and his spouse migrated to Male in the early twelfth century with the consent of the aborigines in the island of Giravaru. Two ships were despatched to Sri Lanka and brought over other people of the 'Lion race' (Sinhalas). Kalaminja was born from this royal couple. He reigned as a Buddhist king for twelve years and afterwards got converted to Islam(Maloney 1980).

Koimala myth as heard by Maloney in Male: The Indian king was angry with his son and banished him with his wife in two boats along with seven hundred followers. They came to Rasgetimu in the atoll of Raa and he became king there. Later on they came to Male and Koimala was born to the Indian couple(Maloney 1980).

Koimala myth in Noon Atoll: When Koimala and his wife came to Maldives, people asked Koimala to rule because of his royal lineage. Koimala brought more people from Sri Lanka. It is said that a beautiful woman named Malakamana from the Maldives was one of the early persons who settled in Sri Lanka (Maloney 1980).

A myth heard by Maloney at Noon Atoll: A hunter king of Sri Lanka caught a man-beast in his net. The king brought him to his residence. The man-beast then married the king's daughter. The king became displeased with the behaviour of the man-beast. The couple was forced to leave Sri Lanka.

They then arrived at Rasgetimu in Maldives. The people of the area requested them to rule(Maloney 1980).

Myth heard in Huludu, Addu Atoll: There was a king in India who was also a hunter. Once he caught a human like creature and took him to the palace. The king discovered some treasures in the forest with the help of this creature. Soon the daughter of the king fell in love with the creature. According to other version the king forced his daughter to marry the creature. However, the king became angry with their behaviour and sent them off on a ship to exile. They came to Male and settled there and later on they started a kingdom (Maloney 1980).

The historicity of Koimala is confirmed in copper-plate inscription which has been found in Maldives.

The above-mentioned stories, rather different versions of a same story, suggest that the islands of Maldives were inhabited by the aboriginal people before the appearance of Koimala and his followers. The ethnic identity of Koimala is obscure but he may represent a generalised ancestral of a royal lineage. It further denotes that the state of monarchy was already formed in Sri Lanka and hence the visiting couple were of an advanced cultural group. Here Koimala and his followers may be considered as pre-Muslim Divehis. In the first version of the same mythical story, it appears that Koimala's parents came from India hence the story identifies Koimala as of Indian origin. The third version of the story, as was heard in Noon Atoll, indicates the link between Sri Lanka and Maldives again. The third and fourth version of the myth are interesting enough because of man-beast concept. Again this man-beast myth can be correlated with the Vijaya myth because Vijaya was the grandson of a lion from which the totemic origin of Sinhala people might have derived. The Koimala story in other version intermingly mixed with Vijaya myth of Sri Lanka as available in the *Mahavamsa*.

Bhutan

The name Bhutan is derived from the Sanskrit word *Bhotanta* i.e., end of Tibet or border land of Tibet (Sinha 1991, Ram Rahul 1971, Chakravarti 1979). The traditional name of Bhutan is *Lho Mon Kha Shi* (Lho Mon Kha Bshi). The people of Bhutan call their country 'Druk Yul' i. e. land of thunder or land of the Druk school of the Kagyupa sect of Buddhism. Bhutan was known as Mon Yul (country of the Mons) when Guru Padmasambhava visited Bhutan in the eighth century A.D. (Chakravarti 1979).

Bhutan is an ancient land of Himalayan kingdom, having a deep-rooted cultural history of its own. But unfortunately source material for depicting the chronological history of Bhutan is inadequate. The authentic chronicles of Bhutan became destroyed due to fire in 1832 (White 1971). The valuable manuscripts also got damaged due to an earthquake in 1897. Hence, the ancient history of Bhutan relies upon some accounts of travellers, the documents left by the East India Company and the British and some surviving manuscripts. A few legends are also available here and there through which one can put some light on history of migration as well as context of relationship between Bhutan and neighbouring countries.

A legendary prince from the kingdom of Sindhu in India who was banished from the country by his father, came to Bhutan and established a kingdom at Bumthang in the eighth century A.D. The Sindhuraja of Bumthang was engaged in a battle with the king of the plains. Nabudara had lost his son in the battle. Being overwhelmed by sorrow and distress, he invited Guru Padmasambhava to Bumthang for propitiation of evil forces and restoration of peace and prosperity. The king and his subjects became his disciples, embraced

Buddhism and regained peace of mind. A boundary pillar was set up between the two kingdoms at mNatong in Khen area. *Sindhu raja-i-Namthar*, the biography of Sindhuraja available in Bhutan, holds that many Indians came and settled down in Bumthang and Punakha during this time (Chakravarti 1980).

The Koch Associated with Bhutan

The Koch, associated with Kamrup and Koch Bihar, also have a claim of historical affiliation to Bhutan. One Sangaldip, a Koch, was said to be king of Kamrup and eastern Bhutan. Sailpati was a Koch king ruling over Bhutanese territories. His son Bisva Singh ruled Kamrup from 1496 to 1553 A.D. It appears that by the end of his reign, Bisva Singh had lost Bhutanese territories to the Tibetan immigrants. It is reported that two sons of Bisva Singh, Naranarayan and Chila Roy, fought among themselves and the latter fled away to Bhutan hills.

> "It is important to notice that the rise of the Koch dynasty to political pre-eminence with their metropolis at Koch Bihar roughly coincided with the expulsion of the Koch tribe from Bhutan by Tibetan under Dharma Raj... However, the historical fact of long struggle between the Koch and the Bhutanese for primacy over the plains of the Duars has a ring of continuity with the earlier confrontation of these two people in the territory of Bhutan"
>
> (Deb 1976).

Nepal

Nepal, a Hindu country lying in the Himalayan range was very much influenced by Buddhist philosophy. In fact, according to myth of Nepal, Buddha is the ninth avtar of Lord Vishnu. Thus Buddha was present in different mythical periods (*Satya, Treta, Dwapar*) and mythical history of Nepal, before the coming of Gautama.

Nepal is very much rich in the Buddhist chronicles. Jatakas, the ancient stories of the previous lives of Buddha, are very much popular in Nepal as well as in India. The origin and the progress of Buddhism is confusing as various mythological legends have mixed up with early history.

Beside the relation of India with Nepal in the epic period, linkages can also be traced in many other stories of Jatakas. In earlier time the Kathmandu valley of Nepal was famous as a huge lake where emerged the *Swayambhu* light. Many ascetics from China, Tibet and India visited this place. Manjusri, according to the Buddhist and Vishnu, according to the Hindus, has been given the credit of transforming the lake into a fertile plain by cutting a pass through the mountains with their swords(Vansittart 1992).

Kashyapa Muni came to Nepal from Benaras and preached the people and went to Gour country (Bengal). He then directed Prachand Deva, a king of Bengal, to go to Nepal. Shaki Deva, the son of Prachand Deva went to Nepal and after assuming the coming of *Kali Yuga* he covered the *Swayambhu* light with a stone and built a *chaitya* and temple over it. He also built five rooms named Basupur, Agripur, Bayupur, Nagpur and Santipur.

The free thinkers like Kashyapa Muni, Kanaka Muni, Sikhi Buddha and others came to Nepal via India and blended the Buddhist and Hindu religion resulting in a distinct culture which finds expression in temples and *chaityas* (Thapa 1981).

It is understood that the history of Nepal before 500 A.D. and 600 A.D. are based on legends and myths. The Kirati, originally dwelling on the eastern part of Nepal, conquered Nepal. After some period they were driven out by Raja Dharma Dutta of Conjeveram of India. He built the temple

Pashupati. It is also believed that this king brought people belonging to the four hindu castes to nepal. (Northey and Morris 1974).

Vikramaditya of Ujjain also came to Nepal. He was succeeded by his son Vikrama Kesari, who caused his son Mandeva to sacrifice him. Mandeva built a Buddhist temple, which exists to this day and is called Bodhnath(Vansittart 1992).

The early history of Nepal is purely based on oral tradition and on myths. Ne Muni, from whom Nepal derives its name, installed the son of a pious cowherd as king and started the cowherd (Gopala) dynasty. The last king of this dynasty, Yaksha Gupta, had no issue. An Ahir, named Bara Simha, from the plains of India came and ruled over the country. This dynasty was conquered by the Kiratis, who came from the east. The Kirata is a well-known tribal name in ancient India. During Jitedasti, the seventh king of this dynasty, Sakya Simha (Buddha) came to Nepal. This king also associated himself with the Pandavas in the great war of Mahabharata. During the reign of Stunko, the fourteenth king of this dynasty, the Emperor Ashoka came to Nepal. The last Kirati king, Gasti was conquered by a kshatriya prince from India named Nimisha. The last king, Bhaskara Varma, of this dynasty was overthrown by the Lichchavis and the authentic history of Nepal begins with the Lichchavi conquest. (Vansittart 1992, Singh Gunanand 1995, Northey & Morris 1974, Majumdar 1952).

The relation of Nepal with India could be traced back from the Epic Age. Valmiki's Ramayana has left a deep impression in the minds of Nepali people. Sita, the daughter of Janaka, lived in Janakpur, situated in Terai region of Nepal. There are some other places in Nepal related to Ramayana. Sitamarhi, thirty miles south-west from Janakpur, is beleived to be the place where marriage of Sita was arranged. Panaura, three miles south west of Sitamarhi, is where new born Sita had been found by the King Janaka while he was ploughing the field. Dhenuka is the place, six miles away from Janakpur, where the broken *dhanus*(bow) was believed to have been kept. Every year a fair is arranged in the place in regard of that (De1976).

At Bhaktapur there is a place called Hanumad Ghat where Valmiki was supposed to have lived for some time, hence the *Siva Linga* of this place is called as Valmikeswera (Varma 1972) The tribe Chepang of Nepal believe in their mythical origin, according to which they are the descendants of Lava, the son of Lord Rama (Gautam & Thapa Magar 1994).

The *Mahabharata* is another great epic highly popular in Nepal. It is so popular in Nepal that one range of Himalaya that encircles the country is called Mahabharata Range. Pashupatinath temple, built by an Indian king was associated with the story of Arjuna's penance and receipt of the Pashupata weapon from Lord Mahadeva, who was in the form of a Kirati. Arjuna obtained the weapon by pleasing Mahadeva with his skill in archery. There is a *linga* called Kirateswara near Pashupati shrine (Varma 1972). In the period of Mahabharata, a Kirati king of Nepal went to Kuruskhetra war by the order of Arjuna to fight against Kauravas. Viratnagar, another legendary place mentioned in the Mahabharata, where Pandavas stayed for a year in incognito from escaping the Kauravas, is also believed to be situated in Nepal. The Rajbansi tribe of Nepal claim to have originated from the Koches. They also believe that Kichak, a king who fought against the Pandavas in Kuruskhetra war, belonged to their tribe. Bhimma, the herculean Pandava ultimately slew Kichak in the area called Kichakbad where the Rajbansis live at present (Gautam & Thapa Magar 1994).

It is said that at the *swayamvara* ceremony of Nala and Damayanti, a king of Nepal was present to witness the event.

It has already been narrated that mythical stories, Jataka tales, epic poems and chronicles relate some linkages among the population of different SAARC countries beginning from ancient period. Jataka tales and Buddhist chronicles linked India, Nepal, Bhutan, Sri Lanka and Maldives. Through epic poem of the *Ramayana* India, Nepal and Sri Lanka are related and the other epic, the *Mahabharata* linked both India and Nepal as well. The chronicles of the *Mahavamsa* and the *Kulavamsa* have shown the relation between India and Sri Lanka. The mythical stories of *Skandapurana* relates India and Sri Lanka and through the folk tales of Koimala stories India and Maldives are linked.

Through Art and Architecture

Study of art and architecture is an important area in the interpretation of cultural heritage. Art is an important aspect of any cultural tradition inherited through generations. Radhakamal Mukherjee defined art as "the metaphysical reality that in its imaginative form or image becomes accessible to man for his contemplation, worship and artistic treatment" (Mukherjee 1984). He further denoted "Indian art, the profundity, beauty and variety of its sculpture, has been effective and fitting vehicle for the spread of Indian culture abroad" (ibid 1984).

Painting and engraving on the walls are the earliest communication of man in the form of art. With the passage of time, number of materials and medias have been used as base or ground for painting. When man lived in caves they painted on rock surface with indigenous colours available around them. The Indus Valley Civilisation left a domain of high art and long artistic tradition behind.

Bithichitra (wall painting) is an example of ancient Indian painting from the first to the tenth centuries. These paintings have been found in the rock temples of Ellora, Badami, Bagh,

Sittan navasal, Ajanta and Jogimara. Such type of paintings have been found in Sigiriya in Sri Lanka (Smith 1911).

The art of scroll painting in India has a hoary antiquity. Scroll painting is the most ancient form of art still continuing in India and its neighbouring countries. The Indian scroll painting was popularly known as *Chitrapata* or *pata*. It served both secular and sacred function depending upon presentation. When it depicted the epic stories as a source of entertainment, its function was secular, but it mostly narrated the life of Buddha and Jataka tales in the religious platform.

The study of development of Indian art is a very difficult task until more data is available. We can only speculate various possibilities of development. It is important to note that most of the monuments were made of either wood or other perishable material which left no trace behind. Art and architecture of India in the ancient period followed trade and religious mission. The art tradition of India reached different parts of South and South-East Asia along with epic themes or through religious tradition, because all these metaphysical episodes like Jataka tales, Avadanas, the Ramayana, the Harivansa and the Mahabharata are acceptable to the people. These art traditions were always patronised by the royal families of ancient India.

The narrative form of art related to Jataka tales and epic poems travelled to South and South-East Asia with the Indian colonisers and missionaries from the early centuries of the Christian era. During the period of Pala and Kushana, the zeal of the Buddhist missionaries helped in spread of Buddhism and Indian culture among the neighbouring countries. The two major religions – the Hinduism and the Buddhism were of Indian origin and entered, Maldives, Nepal, Bhutan and Sri Lanka. The ancient Indian artists also migrated along with traders and religious preachers to these countries. Sometimes, the religious images or reliefs were also taken along with them. From the literary as well as archaeological evidences it can be assumed that there was flow of artists within the Indian subcontinent. The earlier phases of this art was wholly Indian in character, and many early temples and images appear to be the work of Indian artists and craftsmen who migrated from India. Gradually different local styles evolved without loosing the original Indian character.

Bhutan

Like other countries Bhutanese art tradition could be traced in its art forms. G.N. Mehra defined Bhutanese art as *sadhana* like Indian and Tibetan art (Mehra 1974). Bhutan was famous for its artistic production on brass and bronze, though gold, silver and copper items were also made side by side. In earlier period Buddhist art of high excellence reached Bhutan accompanied with religion and philosophy. Varanasi, a cultural spot in India was popular for intertwining gold and silver into artistic designs known as Ganga-Jamuna art in India. Nagendra Singh believes that such particular excellence flourished in Thimpu and Paro in Bhutan in the ancient times with some modification in setting and pattern (Singh 1972). He further pointed out that there were traces of Indian influence on bronze casting for which Bhutan was famous. "There were three varieties associated with Indian bronzes, namely Sharli, U-li and Nupli which originated respectively in eastern, central and western India. The beautiful yellow bronze called Kadam Lima was introduced in the eleventh century A.D. by an Indian Saint" (ibid 1972).

Singh also referred that sandalwood statues of India were specially sent to some of the shrines in Bhutan as objects of worship. Even the craftsmen specialised in woodwork were called from Koch Bihar and employed for wood carving in the Thimpu Dxong (Singh 1968).

The arts and crafts of Sikkim and Bhutan have a close resemblance. With the spread of Buddhism in this land, certain amount of Indian influence came in. Buddhist art had already reached a high degree of excellence in India, the country of its origin. When Buddhism came to Bhutan, it came as a doctrine, belief and philosophy along with highly developed art form, as visual aids in a comprehensive form (Mehra 1974).

Printing and Painting : The Bhutanese art of printing indicates the early history of this region. The ancient copies of Bhutanese print are now in the Bhutan Museum.

The traditional art of painting depicted in the rock monastery of Bumda is situated in the north valley of Paro. The Bhutanese artists were famous for their wall paintings and religious scroll paintings known as *Tankas*. In *Tanka* paintings goddess Tara, Guru Padmasambhava and Lord Buddha are the most popular themes. A few wall paintings depict the legends of Buddha's life and the events leading to *Nirvana* by a brahmin of Bengal. This is a clear indication of Indian influence on art as well as religious philosophy. Singh further mentioned "The technique of applying colours on the walls as well as the line drawings and composition of figures are essentially derived from the Ajanta method, and these basic principles of the Ajanta school are to be found in Bhutan as well"(Singh 1972).

Architecture : In the early part of the seventh century, the Buddhist missionaries laid the foundations of the Buddhist temples in the eastern Himalayas. From the description of the fort of Paro given by Eden, Nagendra Singh opines that these huge mountain fortresses, carved out in the Himalayas, were somewhat simple and straightforward in their architecture compared to the complicated designs which Indian forts displayed, particularly those built in the middle ages such as the famous fortress of Daulatabad, Asirgarh and Ranthambore.

(Singh 1972). The architectural features of stupa of Bhutan became complex though their basic function is the same as they originated from Indian stupa. The best known *chortens* of Bhutan have been built which are akin to the plan of the ancient stupa of Sarnath (Mehra 1974).

The aforesaid information on Bhutanese art and architecture reveals that there are clear indication of Indian influence. The great philosophy of Buddhism reached this country as a form of religion along with the art form related to this religion simultaneously. There was flow of artists along with the missionaries. Some of the art forms reached this land of Himalaya without any change and some became modified as per need.

Sri Lanka

Sri Lanka has been the home of vital and enduring art. The remains of this notable art are found in the ruined temples and palaces, walls and ceilings of the caves and in the exposed niches of Sigiriya.

The ancient art of Sri Lanka has remarkable link with the art of India. The Tamil invaders brought with them their artists and builders. The Sinhalese art flourished with the blend of Indian concepts of religion and indigenous Sinhalese genius. Wikramasinghe in his book, *Aspect of Sinhalese Culture* admits that Sinhalese borrowed many cultural elements from India. But the borrowed elements changed in the process of adaptations.

Coomaraswamy, a Tamil scholar and research fellow in Indian, Iranian and Mohammedan art at the Boston Museum of Fine Arts, believed that the art of Sri Lanka was distinctly Indian, without influence of Greece or Rome, and that maturing independently, it exerted influence on the Gupta art of India and became the model for the Buddhist art which spread eastward from Sri Lanka. The ancient art of Sri Lanka was mostly based on religious ideology and theme. The paintings as well as the architecture were dedicated to Buddhism, during the ascendancy of the Sinhalese king. The arts were developed under the patronage of the kings or of the Buddhist clergy.

According to Harle (1986) "Sri Lanka is nonetheless an ancient and distinct cultural entity. It is the only country in South and South East Asia to have remain predominantly Buddhist since the days of Ashoka, and Buddhism has been the principle influence on its culture, its art and its architecture".

The first major *dagabas* (Buddhist shrine)was the Thuperama, built in Anuradhapura in 307 B.C. by the King Tissa after his conversion to Buddhism. It is said to be the oldest Buddhist shrine of either India or Sri Lanka. Jetawanarama of Polonnaruwa was the temple of Buddha in mixed Indian and Sinhalese styles (Tresidder 1960).

The reign of the first great king Devanampiya Tissa (250 - 210 B.C.) saw the reception of Mahindra and the establishment of the first stupa (Sinhalese *dagaba*) at Anuradhapura. According to the chronicles, the Rajamahavihara at Mihintale was erected over the ashes of the great missionary, Mahindra. (Harle 1986). Sri Lanka's *dagaba* rests on a tripleringed or terraced base at the foot of the hemispherical dome. The projection of four corners prove close early link with Andhra.

A rock-cut colossus at Avukana, 46 ft. high with its flame-shaped finial was made on the *usnisa** in the eighth century.

---

* It simply means 'peak', 'top' but Buddha's usnisa is derived from the topknot in which the uncut hair of a member of the warrior caste, whence the Buddha came, was worn under the turban.

The thirteen century rock-cut sculptures of the Gal Vihara at Polonnaruwa gives a clear style of late Gupta period.

In Annuradhapura and Polonnaruwa there are large number of Buddhist sculptures. The style is closely related to the sculptures of Amaravati of Andhra Pradesh. The most impressive of this is the colossal image, nearly fifty feet long of the Buddha's death or *Nirvana* at the Gal Vihara at Polonnaruwa.

Detached Bodhisattva head from the Thumparama (now in Colombo museum) and the standing Buddhas of third or fourth century A.D. now in Anuradhapura Museum, are examples of linkage with Amaravati.

Rock-cut Pallava sculpture shows most beautiful instinct with the understanding of animal behaviour. For instance, in Sri Lanka elephants were sported among lotuses in a bath near the Tisaveva lake at Isurumuni (Harle 1986).

With the establishment of Buddhism in Sri Lanka, artist came from India during the kingship of Ashoka to depict the life and work of Buddha. As Ananda Coomaraswamy has pointed out that early Buddhist art was "popular, sensuous, animistic Indian art adapted to the purpose of the illustration of Buddhist anecdote and the decoration of the Buddhist monuments" (cf Tresidder 1960).

The Ajanta style of paintings are found in the great boulder mountain of Sigiriya. It was a fortress-cum palace. The rock face of the gallery leading to the summit was painted in tempera with the famous *apsaras* in a style of contemporary frescos at Ajanta.

Paranavitana, the Sri Lankan archaeologist, is of the opinion that the artists of Sigiriya and Ajanta "shared the ideals of the Indian painters but their treatment of the feminine form differed in detail" between Duttagamini and Elara. There are historical scenes like the landing of Vijaya and the duel depicted on the walls of the rock temple at

Dambulla (Tresidder 1960). Tresidder also wrote that "Ceylonese painting in its period of distinction, unquestionably a lineal descendant of Indian paintings, developed its own characteristic style that kept its vitality after Indian painting declined" (Tresidder 1960). Coomaraswami says "Sinhalese art is of particular value in preserving early Hindu feeling which in most parts of the mainland has been replaced by Mohammedan or later Hindu motifs. Sinhalese decorative is, thus in a sense, both freer and wider than that of northern India in later times, and gentler, less grotesque, more akin to medieval European, than the Dravidian art of southern India, to which it is, nevertheless, so closely related" (cf Tresidder 1960).

Scroll paintings are rare in Sri Lanka. Though almost parallel to the scroll paintings of India and Nepal of South-East Asia, *Bali* painting is popular in Sri Lanka.

Prehistoric findings of certain part of Sri Lanka like Balangoda have shown some resemblance of culture between Sri Lanka and India even during 10,000 to sixth century B.C. Skeletal remains and some implements of stone and bone unearthed at 'Balangoda culture' reveal that the Balangoda man had Australoid characteristics and lived in caves (C.R. De Silva 1987). The Balangoda man seems to have acquired some knowledge of agriculture, the art of pottery, the ability of shaping stone tools and techniques of drilling. Their culture resembled to that of the people of neighbouring south India and there was probably considerable interaction across the Palk Straits (C.R. De Silva 1987).

Another archaeological evidence found from excavations made at Pomparippu in north-west Sri Lanka shows that the south Indian megalithic culture had considerable influence over that region of the island at least by the third century B.C. De Silva 1987 De Silva 1981). The style of urn burials, the pottery and the associated objects found in Pomparippu are similar to objects found at the Adichchanallur site across the Gulf of Mannar in India.

Maldives

The linkage of Maldives through art and architecture with Indian-subcontinent is not very much clear because of non-availability of archaeological and other related material in this context. Proper interpretation and study of the available material are also pending. Buddhism reached this island-country before the Islamic period along with related art and architecture as we find in other Buddhist countries of South Asia. The Buddhist monuments and associated art objects found in Maldives have not been analysed and interpreted so far.

From the H.C.P. Bell's mission in 1922 it was reported that in Maldives there are baring sand dunes on a few islands. But in several islands there are hemispherical mounds covered with fifteen to eighteen feet high soil. The local people recognise these as being monuments related to Buddhism. These are stupas, hemispherical structures of coral stone, containing a small casket or two with relics of Buddhist saints. (Maloney 1980).

It was also noted that the most impressive archaeological remains of Buddhism have been seen on the larger islands in the southern part. In Seenu there was a stupa and a Bodhi tree but the British bulldozed the stupa when they made an airstrip there.

However, these islands had developed the art of shipbuilding at the early stage of civilisation.

Nepal

The traditional linkages of arts and crafts between India and Nepal had been established through traders, priests or monks who visited both the countries for the propagation of religion under the patronage of the kings who immigrated to Nepal in earlier periods. A large number of artists also travelled to Nepal for the propagation of Indian religions through illustrative material including the iconography of a very large number of sculptures and paintings.

The valley of Kathmandu is full of marvellous stupas, beautiful pagodas with their magnificent pillars and excellent Buddhist images. Nepal has shown a high degree of development in art and architecture and the Newar tribe had their contribution with regard to craftsmanship. The Newars adapting their own ideas along with Indian style produced the typical architectural feature with a special character of its own.

Archaeological remains suggest that the earlier relations of Nepal with India started from the third century B.C. when Emperor Ashoka raised a well-known pillar in Kathmandu valley at Lumbini marking the birth place of Buddha. Ashoka also visited Kathmandu and built four stupas at Lalitpur. Archaeological excavations at Telanukot, Banjarahi and Paisia in the Tarai region indicate the cultural sequence with Mauryas, Sungas, Kushanas and Guptas according to the Indian historical and archaeological terminology. (Varma 1972).

It is apparent that the Indian artists had travelled to Nepal for the propagation of religions through illustrative materials. The main religious architectures are Buddhist stupas, *chaitya-viharas* and Brahmanical temples.

The report of Hiuen-Tsang in 657 A.D. described that the houses and temples of Nepal had the presence of towers with many tiers and were carved with wooden doors and windows. These buildings were called secular buildings and were originally made of wood and got resemblances with early Indian reliefs. It is also clear that religious architecture was nothing but transition to stone of what was originally made in wood. (Varma 1972).

The art of Tarai region of Nepal forms a continuity with that of north India, particularly with regard to terracotta and stone sculpture. The terracotta objects of animal and human figures found in the region date back to Maurya, Kushana and Gupta periods (Encyclopaedia of Asian History 1988).

According to Harle (1986), "a few sculptures of the early Lichchavi period (300-850 A.D.), generally in very poor condition and with close affinities to late Kushana work at Mathura or early Gupta remains in the western Uttar Pradesh, include a pair of Haritis either in a squatting or in Pralambapada pose, and a standing Bodhisattva". Thus links with western rather than eastern are confirmed (Halre 1986).

The distinctive features of the Brahmanical temple in Nepal is the absence of *mandapa* in front of *garbha-griha* except in case of Pashupatinatha temple. The other important Brahmanical temple in Nepal, Yaka-bahi an old temple is situated in Kathmandu and the temple of Siva-Parvati also are of these types.

Brown (1989), noted that a few religious edifices are to be seen of the typically Hindu character as in India and according to Fergusson's view "a square tower like temple with a perpendicular base, but a curvilinear outline above". This style of building indicates the spiritual link connected with India (Brown 1989).

The extensive architecture of western Nepal particularly in Karnali basin is significant. This area developed in Khas empire in medieval period. The temples are influenced from Kumaon region of India with modest proportion and are in the plain *sikhara* style (Encyclopedia of Asian History 1988). The distinctive style of temple built in stone or brick with sharp-edged pyramidal tower shows the Nepalese modification of Indian *sikhara*. The best example of this modification can be seen in the Krishna temple of Patan. Another example of Indian *sikhara* type is the Mahabandha temple of Bodhgaya. In Latikaili temple the ground plan is rectangular and is covered by a roof of the curvilinear hut type of Bengal with rectangular veranda in front. From the inscription it suggests that the architect came from Benaras (Varma 1972).

Due to the constant interaction between the two countries India and China, the architecture of Nepal got very much influenced in various times. "During the Buddhist period, the inhabitants of the valley looked to India for inspiration and guidance and the buildings of this early time are the solid stone order in the manner of "Chaityas" and "Stupas" of the great teacher's native country" (Brown 1989). The architecture of Nepal on Buddhist edifices are broadly consigned to two great style the *Chaitya* and the *Pagoda*.

The Buddhist stupas and *chaitya-viharas* in Nepal constitute one single unit of establishment. There are more than two hundred stupas located mainly in Patan and Kathmandu. The monasteries are sometimes double-storeyed and follow invariably the general plan in India, that consist of a square block formed by four rows of walls arranged along the four sides of an inner quardrangle. (Varma 1972).

The oldest stupas in Nepal are the Ashokan stupas in Patan and these remind of the typical Mauryan stupas of India. The Svayambhunatha shrine and the shrine dedicated to Manjusri situated in Sangu are also famous stupas. According to R.S. Varma "The plan of Svayambhunatha is that of the usual stupa characteristic of the valley. It is a square temple over which rises an up-turned saucer like tumulus surmounted by a square box like construction responding evidently to the Buddhist *harmika*, on the four carrdinal faces of which are four enormous human eyes looking out into the external world as it were. This decoration on the four cardinal sides of the *harmika* seems to be characteristic feature of Nepalese stupa shrines." (Varma 1972).

Nepal contributes significantly in respect of art of bronze casting in Asia. But there is no doubt that these arts and crafts were first learnt by the craftsmen of Nepal from Indian masters which were improved subsequently. The earliest pieces of bronze sculptures are of the Lichchavi period, but the art of bronze casting reached its peak in the thirteenth and fourteenth centuries. From archaeological evidences it is revealed that the important centres of bronze casting in eastern India were located in Nalanda, Kurkihar in Bihar and other places of Bengal. (Varma 1972 and Encyclopaedia of Asian History 1988).

The Nepal school of painting as also the unconventional Tibetan painting of the yellow sect, are allied to the Gujarati and Pala schools in pictorial arrangement and design. (Regmi 1975).

Painting in Nepal belong to the well-known Pala style and form of manuscript paintings in Bengal and Bihar in the tenth century onwards. Nepal has also been a cornucopia of paintings on mural palm-leaf and paper manuscripts. *Pata* or *pata* paintings show influence of Pala school and form of manuscript paintings. The most important illustrated manuscript of the *Ashtasahasrika Prajnaparamita* and another important illustrated manuscript of *Panchrkaha* was done by the artists from Gangetic region. One manuscript of the Prajnaparamita is now in the custody of the Asiatic Society, Calcutta and dated equivalent to 1071 A.D. (Varma 1972).

Indian subcontinent has a rich cultural heritage from the early age. The Indus Valley civilisation left a domain of high art and long artistic tradition behind. The art tradition of India migrated to different parts of South and South-East Asia. The early remains of art of sculpture have been traced back to Mauryan, Sungan and Kushana period. The famous art style of Gandhara were found from Kushana period in the first century A.D. The tremendous influence of art flourished in the Gupta period and got distributed throughout India and outside. In later period, various art styles or school of art originated in different parts of India following Gupta tradition.

122 Populations of the SAARC Countries: Bio-cultural Perspectives

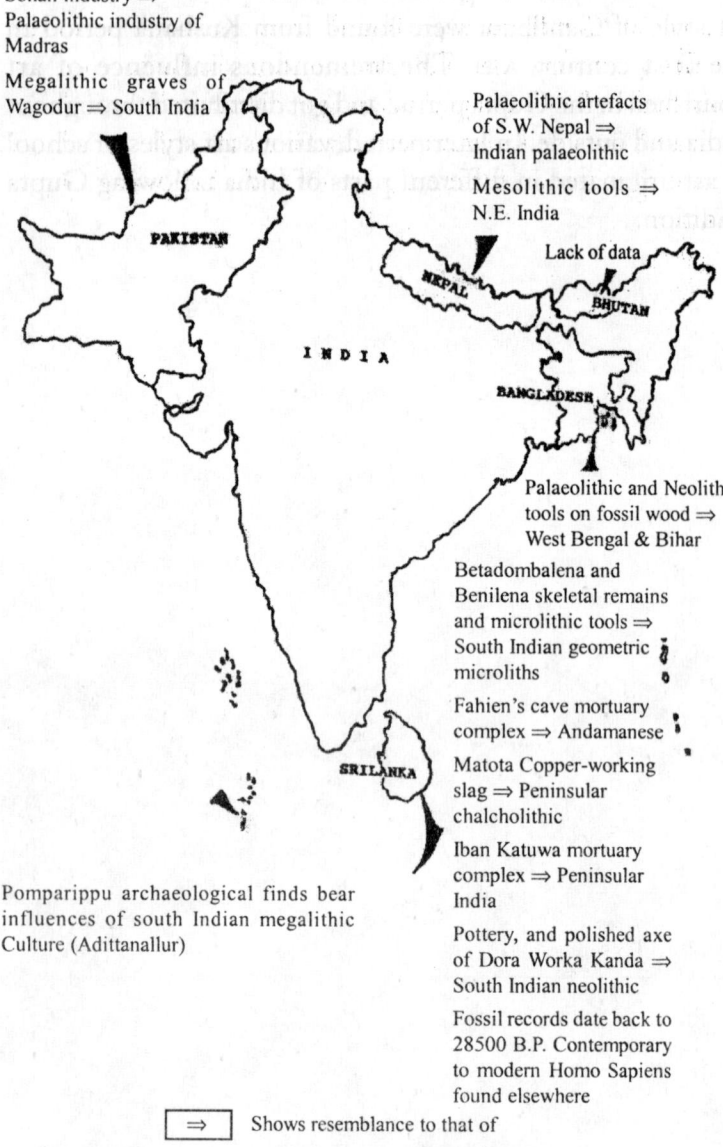

Map-2: Similarities of the SAARC Countries in Prehistoric archaeology.

Cultural Linkages Among the People...

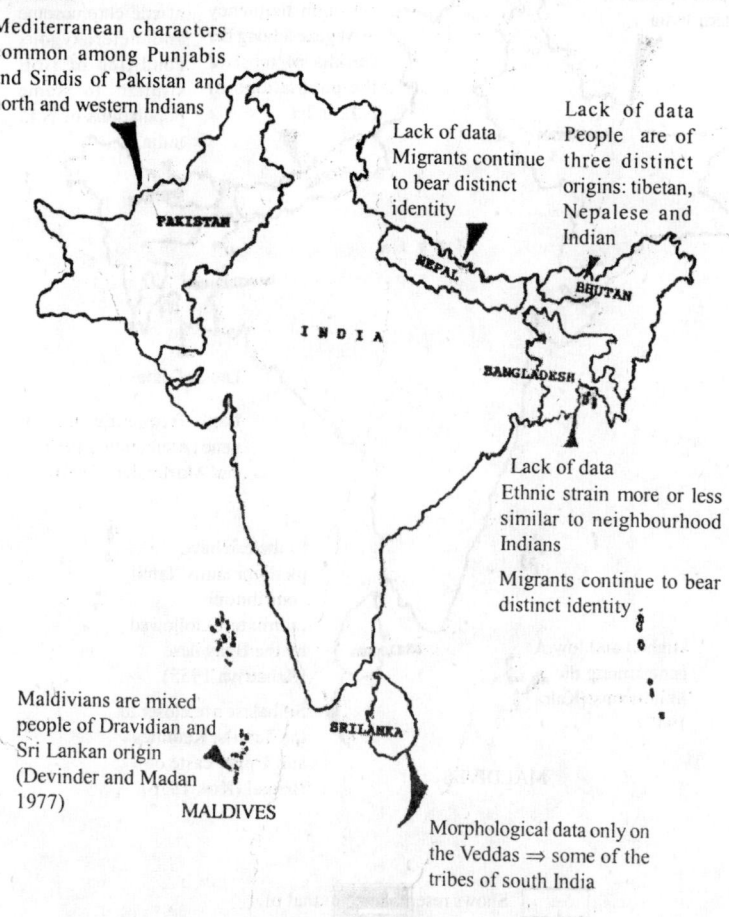

Nordic elements found among the Pathan of Pakistan ⇒ Kashmiris, Punjabis and Coorgis of India

Brachycephalic element in Baluchistan and Sind ⇒ Gujarat, Maharashtra, Karnataka

Mediterranean characters common among Punjabis and Sindis of Pakistan and north and western Indians

Lack of data
Migrants continue to bear distinct identity

Lack of data
People are of three distinct origins: tibetan, Nepalese and Indian

Lack of data
Ethnic strain more or less similar to neighbourhood Indians

Migrants continue to bear distinct identity

Maldivians are mixed people of Dravidian and Sri Lankan origin (Devinder and Madan 1977)

Morphological data only on the Veddas ⇒ some of the tribes of south India

⇒ Shows resemblance to that of

Map-3: Similarities of the people of the SAARC Countries in morphological characters.

124 Populations of the SAARC Countries: Bio-cultural Perspectives

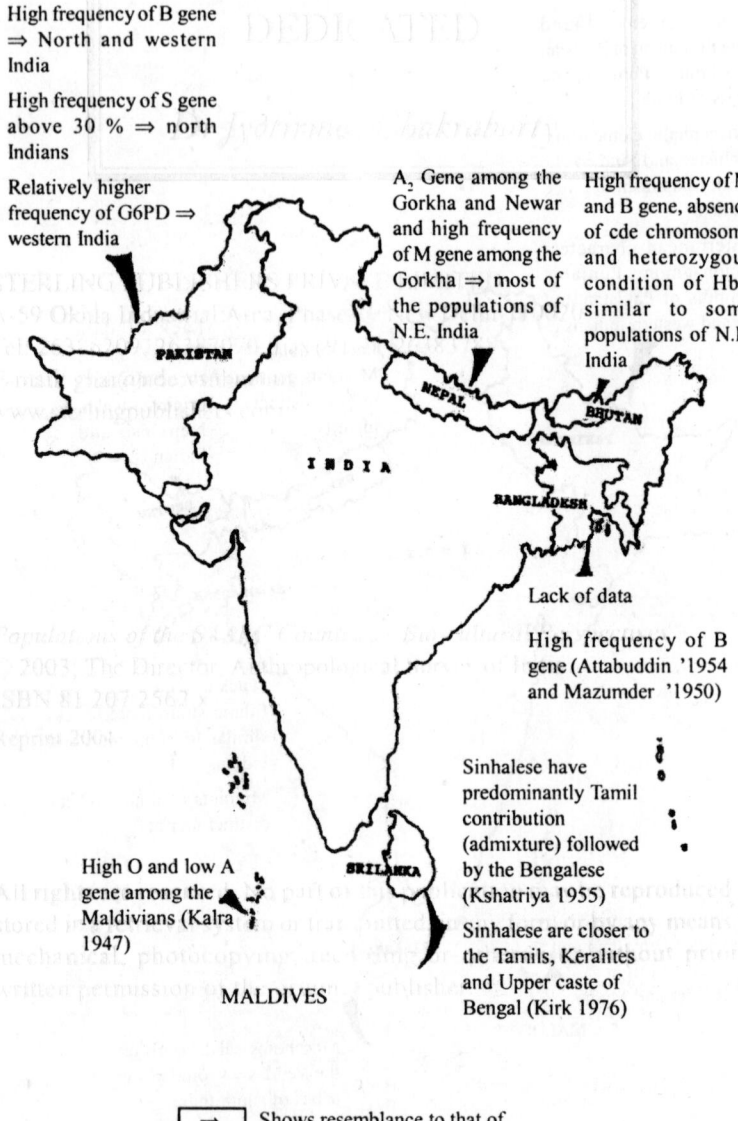

High frequency of B gene ⇒ North and western India

High frequency of S gene above 30 % ⇒ north Indians

Relatively higher frequency of G6PD ⇒ western India

A_2 Gene among the Gorkha and Newar and high frequency of M gene among the Gorkha ⇒ most of the populations of N.E. India

High frequency of M and B gene, absence of cde chromosome and heterozygous condition of HbE similar to some populations of N.E. India

Lack of data

High frequency of B gene (Attabuddin '1954 and Mazumder '1950)

Sinhalese have predominantly Tamil contribution (admixture) followed by the Bengalese (Kshatriya 1955)

High O and low A gene among the Maldivians (Kalra 1947)

Sinhalese are closer to the Tamils, Keralites and Upper caste of Bengal (Kirk 1976)

MALDIVES

⇒ Shows resemblance to that of

Map-4: Similarities of the people of the SAARC Countries in blood groups and cell enzyme.

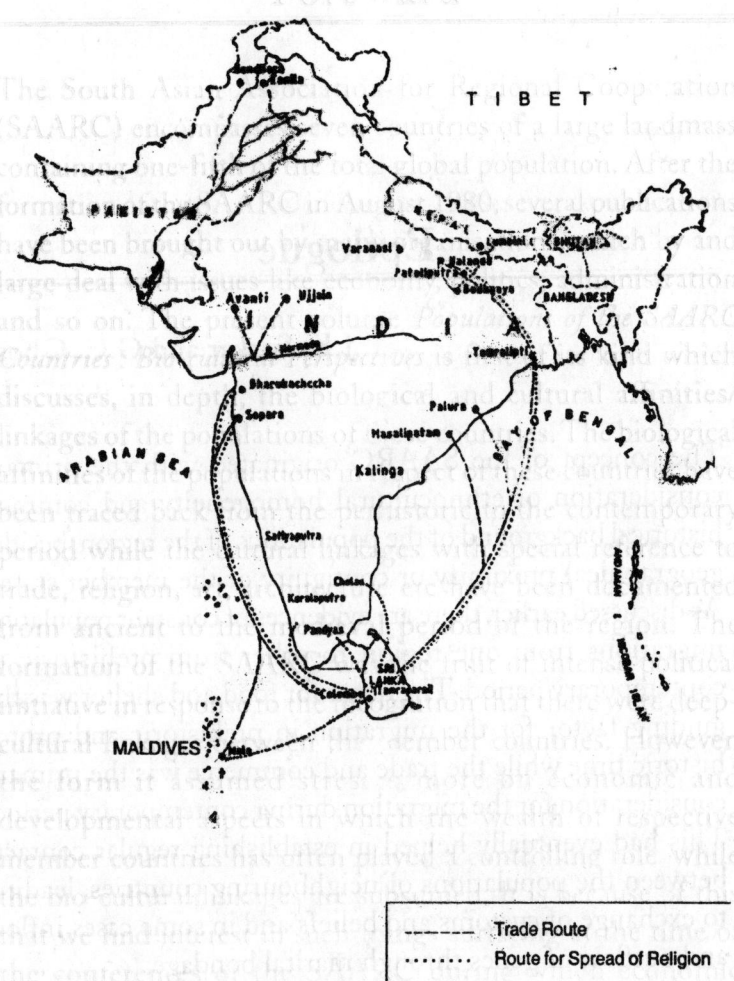

Map-5: Spread of religion and trade in the SAARC Countries.

Epilogue

J.K. Sarkar and G.C. Ghosh

The concept of the SAARC originated with the primary consideration of ethnocultural homogeneity and common historical background of the populations of the region, besides geographical proximity or contiguity of the member states. As discussed earlier, there are evidences of constant population migrations from one region to other from prehistoric to contemporary period. The quest for food and shelter was the guiding factor for the migration in prehistoric and protohistoric time while the trade and commerce was the primary consideration for the migration during contemporary period. This had eventually helped in establishing regular contacts between the populations of neighbouring countries, leading to exchange of customs and beliefs and in some cases inflow and outflow of genes through marital bondage.

The information related to such bio-cultural homogeneity of the population of the SAARC countries are available sporadically in literature and old records which sometimes remain unnoticed. The present exercise is an attempt to compile such information from the available resources comprehending the situation that may help in reinforcing and renewing the age-old relationship of the populations of Sri Lanka, Pakistan, Maldives, Bangladesh, Bhutan and Nepal.

Epilogue

The task of drawing biological linkages seems to be difficult while cultural linkages are relatively conspicuous. In order to understand the extent of gene flow one has to take into account the identity of the ethnic groups which are not decipherable in available records. Historical and other records demonstrate that there has been population mixing due to migration but it is difficult to surmise the identity of populations which were actually involved in such marital contact. Besides that, the geophysical, environment and ecological conditions play an important role in shaping the biological features, particularly the morphology that induce homogeneity in physical characters among the populations of a region cutting across the political boundary. Above all, the migratory groups have quite often lost their identities baring a few cases e.g. in Nepal, Bangladesh, Pakistan and Sri Lanka where the groups which have migrated from India in recent past continue to maintain their ethnic identities. Being faced with the problems of population identity, the present exercise is restricted to discuss on population affiliation based on the trend of data set.

Chumki Piplai and J.M. Sarkar have made attempts to present the information on the populations of Sri Lanka, Pakistan, Maldives, Bangladesh, Nepal and Bhutan so far as their migration is concerned to India and vice-versa, from prehistoric to contemporary period in addition to compiling biological data on the concerned populations. Their attempts are based on available records but due to obvious reasons it cannot be claimed as exhaustive. They have mainly dealt with prehistoric, archaeological and biological information such as anthropometry, selected blood groups and in some cases red-cell enzymes to bring into relief the situation of population affinities (Maps 2-4).

The cultural contact of the population of Sri Lanka in the southern part of India is perhaps from prehistoric past as it is evident from the findings of several prehistoric sites in Sri Lanka. Microlithic tools from Beta-Domba-Lena as well as Benilena and pottery and polished axe of Dora Worka Kanda bear strong similarities with the neolithic tools and other artefacts discovered from south India. Pomparippu archaeological findings display strong impact of south Indian megalithic culture found in Adittanallur. Copper-working slag of Matota in Sri Lanka shows resemblances with that of chalcholithic peninsular India. The mortuary complexes unearthed from Fahien's cave and Ibban Katuwa have similarities with those found in peninsular India and among the people of Andaman and Nicobar Islands. The recorded history of movements of Indian populations to Sri Lanka dates back to sixth century B.C. Since then there has been continuous waves of migration of populations in these two countries particularly for trade and commerce and the prominent centres for these merchandise movements from Indian subcontinent were southern and eastern part of the country. History reveals that the Sri Lankans were taken to Kaveri delta by the Cholas in the second century A.D. and the south Indian princes established kingdom in Sri Lanka in the tenth century A.D. Besides, there has been a large-scale migration from Malabar coast of Coromondal in the fifteenth century A.D. Merchant's sail from eastern India to Sri Lanka attain a considerable height and as a result it occupied prominent position in the *Mangalkabya*, *Satyapirer Panchali* or *Sonir Panchali*, the folk literature of West Bengal.

Morphological studies on the population of Sri Lanka are almost negligible. The only group that has been considered for morphological study is the Veddas, the original inhabitant of the Island who bear physical characters similar to those of some tribes of south India. Kirk (1962), Saha (1988), Kshatriya (1995), Papiha et al. (1996) and Mourant (1975) conducted serological and biogenetic studies among the Sinhalese population considering a number of loci in order to find out the genetic distance with the populations of India, those who are historically and culturally close. Though there is lack of uniformity in the inferences that they have arrived at but it is evident that the Sinhalese and the Tamils of Sri Lanka are closer to the Indian Tamils and the south Indian Muslims and the Sinhalese have a predominant Tamil contribution followed by the Bengalese. Kirk (1976) is of the opinion that the "modern Sinhalese populations are closer to the Tamils and the Keralites of south India and the upper caste of Bengal than they are to the population of Gujarat or Punjab."

The population migration between India and Pakistan is a prehistoric phenomenon. The lithic tools of Sohan industry bear much resemblances to choppers and hand axes found in Madras industry. The megalithic graves of Waghdor (Karachi) are indistinguishable from those of Deccan. The neolithic and metal age civilisation derive much from Makran Coast and Baluchistan. The Indus Valley civilisation with its centre at Mohenjo-Daro spread over a large area including western part of India.

Harappa and Addittanallur crania bear common ethnic strains. All these together stand as a testimony of high degree of relationship between the people of India and Pakistan in the sphere of culture and biology from time immemorial.

The anthropometric and serological data so far available from Pakistan show similarities with some of the populations of northern and western India. The Nordic, Mediterranean and Brachycephalic elements commonly found among the Pathans, Baluchis, Sindhis and Punjabis in Pakistan are also reported from some populations of Kashmir and Punjab, Gujarat and Rajasthan as well as Karnataka. Higher frequency of B gene and G6PD are reported from some of the populations of Pakistan as well as from northern and western part of India. High frequency of S gene which is quite often more than 30% is another notable feature found among some of the populations of Pakistan and north India. Cavilli-Saforza (1994) while trying to understand the genetic relationship of the populations of South Asia has observed a small sub-cluster formed by the samples from Pakistan and India which signifies closer biological relationship between the populations of the two countries.

The populations of Maldives show marked affinity with the Sri Lankan populations in terms of their language and physical appearances. It is said that the Maldivians are the descendants of the Veddas, Sinhalese, Dravidians and the Arabs (Ananda 1997). Devinder and Madan (1977) also considered the Maldivians as the mixed people of Dravidian and Sri Lankan origin. There are historical evidences of migration of population to Maldives from India particularly from Kerala, Gujarat and Bangladesh but this is not significant in terms of making any impact on biological characters of the Maldivians. The only study on the serology of the Maldivians was conducted by Kalra (1947) which show high frequency of O gene (58.3 percent) and low frequency of A gene (17.5 percent) which bear similarity with the populations of neighbouring Minocoy Islands (Bhattacharya and Biswas 1978). Like Pakistan, the biological characteristics of Bangaladeshis bear much resemblances with that of the populations living in its neighbouring areas of India. Besides there is number of social groups living in both the countries maintaining one and the same identity. The information on prehistoric Bangladesh is limited to the discovery of fossil-wood implements bearing paleolithic and neolithic characteristics found from southern part of the country. The similar kind of tools have also been unearthed from Chhotanagpur plateau of Bihar and Birbhum district of West Bengal, India. The ethnic elements among Bangaladeshis are of diverse nature and have resemblances to those of Indian populations. Proto-Australoid and Mongoloid are the basic ethnic elements of the tribes of India and Bangladesh. Very little work on biological anthropology has so far been reported from Bangladesh excepting a few studies on the serology (Majumdar 1950, Attabuddin 1954) which show high frequency of B gene which is also a characteristic feature among the populations of contiguous region of India.

The present day populations of Bhutan are said to have three origins i.e. Tibet, Nepal and India. There is lack of data on the biological aspects of the population of Bhutan. Glasgow (1968) reported high frequency of B and M gene among the Bhutanese, which are also, characteristics of most of the populations of India. Besides, absence of cde chromosome and lower frequency of heterozygous E haemoglobin are observed among the Bhutanese bearing similarities with the populations of north-east India.

Nepalese are said to be of Tibetan origin (Hodgson 1940) who are mixed with Indian populations in course of subsequent migration from northern India, particularly from Uttar Pradesh, Bihar and West Bengal. Historical evidences of bio-cultural relationship between the populations of these two countries dates back to Ashoka's time. Besides there are records of trade and commerce which paved the way of smooth transference of bio-cultural elements. Like in Bangladesh, some of the social groups of Nepal and India continue to bear their original identities even after migration bearing the same physical characters. Studies on the biological aspect of the Nepalese are very few. Bird et al. (1957) reported high frequency of A and M gene among the Gorkhas which show similarities with some of the populations of north-east India.

The evidences of prehistoric lithic industry in Nepal are only represented by the discoveries of paleolithic and mesolithic artefacts. The paleolithic tools show similarities with those found in Indian subcontinent in general while the mesolithic tools show resemblances with those found in north-east India.

It is thus evident that there have been a constant flow of population from all the six neighbouring countries to India. This phenomena started from prehistoric past so far as Sri Lanka, Pakistan and Nepal are concerned. But for other countries due to lack of prehistoric or archaeological records, population migration has been traced from historical evidences. The most important factors behind these migrations were trade and commerce besides religion which led to cultural contact. While cultural influence does not imply intermarriages, it is to be borne in mind that the ethnic identities of these groups were not developed strongly enough to keep them distinct. In absence of identities of the ethnic groups which were involved in gene mixing and due to limitation of data there was no option but to go for generalised observation which has been discussed earlier. Morpho-serological information so far available tend to show that the population living in contiguous region irrespective of political boundaries bear more or less similar characteristics. The similarities exhibited by different groups today may be conjectured as the consequence of gene exchange followed by repeated and successful biological adaptation by their ancestors to the changing ecological conditions.

The review of existing literature on the SAARC countries reveals that the population of these countries had maintained cultural linkages even during the ancient and medieval periods. Such linkages are clearly discernible in respect of religion, trade, art and architecture. There are also evidences of prevalence of similar mythical stories that suggest presence of interaction among the people of these countries.

The review further suggests that religion had played a very important role in maintaining such linkages. Some of the literature viewed that religion perhaps reached in some lands through traders or merchants much before the missionaries took the initiative in the spread of religion. The importance of trade and trade routes in establishing religious and cultural linkages cannot be denied. In the ancient and medieval periods, there were a number of trade routes both in land and sea. Number of important ports like Tamralipti, Masulipatam, Bhrigukuchha, Sopara etc. were spread over in different parts of India. A port has been referred to by different names at many occasions because of its association with different areas, for example, Bhrigukuchha is also known as Barygaza or Broach, Tamralipti as Tamluk. An interesting feature appears out of the review of these literature. The Himalayan region where all the neighbouring countries were depended on rock salt of Tibet necessitated Bhutan, Nepal and Sikkim to maintain some linkages through interdependence of trade. A critical appraisal of the literature reviewed indicates that religion had a very significant role to play in the spread of trade or diffusion of cultural traits in countries like Nepal and Bhutan. Buddhism went to Tibet via Nepal. The great Indian monks Shantarakshit, Padmasambhava and Atisa Dipankara had been to Tibet accepting invitation of Tibetan kings. On the way to Tibet they stayed in Nepal with the warm welcome of kings of Nepal. Even one of the princes of Nepal embraced Buddhism and became a disciple of an Indian monk. King of Bhutan invited Guru Padmasambhava for restoration of peace and happiness in that country.

The literature reviewed here, however, do not throw much light with regard to appearance of Buddhism in Maldives. Though there are traces of Buddhist stupas and remnants of Buddhist architecture in that island, it can, however, be stated categorically that Buddhism had reached this island country much before the Islamic faith spread there. The influence of Hinduism can be co-related with the traders of Indian origin whose visits in this island country have been recorded by many scholars.

An examination of information regarding art and architecture available in the literature clearly denotes that there had been a constant flow of artists and art between these countries. Though there were regional variations in the art forms, a commonness underneath these art forms and architecture can hardly be overlooked.

It does not require to mention once again that the populations of the SAARC countries namely Sri Lanka, Maldives, Nepal and Bhutan had cultural linkages with the people of India since the ancient period. However, the literature reviewed in this volume also establish that such cultural linkages were not uniform for all these countries.

Linkages with Sri Lanka were significantly visible, while position of Maldives in this respect was minimum. It is needless to say that such linkages in many respects, were determined by the nature of communication facilities, which had existed between these countries. The geographical proximity of Sri Lanka and Nepal to India may be one of the important factors that encouraged the people of these countries to venture in establishing contacts in the ancient and medieval periods. Even in such case of proximity, the extent of cultural linkages of the people of India with their counterpart in Sri Lanka and Nepal were far from uniform. This leads one to look into the conditions of the communication facilities that these two countries had with India. While the island country of Sri Lanka was approachable only through the water surface transport system along the sea routes, Nepal had a few mountain passes in the Himalayas which could be used for interaction. Adventurous enterpreneurs of India made repeated efforts to reach these countries. Presumably to extend their horizon of trade such enterpreneurs of India had looked at the neighbouring countries like Sri Lanka, Nepal, Bhutan and Tibet at the very first instance. Establishment of trade link normally necessitates involvement of two categories of people, the sellers and the buyers. The transaction between the sellers and the buyers in ancient period, by and large used to take place through exchange of commodities. This naturally demands presence of exchangeable wealth in both the countries. More the availability of the exchangeable wealth, better is the chance of drawing attention of the traders. Exchangeable wealth may be in the form of natural resources or exchangeable currency. In accordance with this simple principle, the trade links with population of India was in greater degree with the people of Sri Lanka.

It is evident from the historical records that Sri Lanka was very famous for its natural wealth like gems and good quality pearls. These attracted the traders from neighbouring countries from very early part of history. Kautilya referred to pearl as *Tamraparnika* which used to be produced only in Tamraparni or ancient Ceylon. On the other hand, silver and copper were not available in that country as per their requirement. Sastri (1952) observed that Ceylon was depended on India for silver and copper, as these metals were not produced in Ceylon. It may be mentioned that the earliest coins of Ceylon were akin to those of India. Similarly rice and raw materials of textiles were not sufficiently available in the island country which used to be transported from Bengal through river and sea routes by the traders. It may be pointed out that Bengal at that period was famous in production of rice and textiles.

Table - 1 : Trade – Extent of trade link of India with other SAARC nations

	Location	Routes of communication	Availability of exchangeable commodities	Required exchangable commodities	Remarks
Sri Lanka	Nearer to India	Sea and river routes	Rich in pearls and gems	Lack in silver, rice and cotton	Attracted traders from Gujarat, Bengal. High degree of trade link
Nepal	-do-	Mountain passes	Lack of commodities	---	Involved as trans-Himalayan traders between Tibet and India. Functioned as bridge community.
Bhutan	-do-	Mountain passes/ corridors	Mask, yak's tail, rugs	Areca nut, silk	Trade link limited to Tarai region. Traders of Kamrupa and Bhutan had limited exchange through barter
Maldives	Relatively distantly located	Sea routes surrounded by dangerous coral reefs. Difficult to approach.	No evidence of availability of exchangable commodities	---	Less attractive to the traders. Insignificant trade link

Contrary to this situation, the Himalayan kingdom of Nepal lacked in natural resources excepting some forest produces. The varieties of trees grown in Nepal had a great demand in India owing to their strength and durability. However, linkages with the people of Nepal was mainly continued since the strategic position of the country between India and Tibet facilitated Nepal to act as bridge nation. Tibet was rich in natural wealth like gold and precious gems, masks and yaks' tail. These items were in great demand among the people of India which could be obtained from Tibet only through the people of Nepal. From the very early time Nepal thus became very actively engaged in trans – Himalayan trade with Tibet and plains of India.

The nature of trade link between the people of India and Sri Lanka and those of Nepal was clearly different. While the traders of India could directly establish trade linkages with Sri Lankan population, the linkage with Nepal was restricted only at the level of 'middle man' between Tibet and India. The traders, who used to visit Sri Lanka with their commodities, probably had considered it convenient to spend longer period in that country in order to earn more wealth. In absence of similar situation, establishment of such linkages were not very much possible with the people of Nepal.

The distant location of Maldives from India together with the dangerous coral reefs that surround the islands in all probability, did not encourage the traders in large number to make attempt in establishing trade linkage with this island people. However, the traders from Gujarat did reach to these islands as apparent from the defunct Gujarati norms and customs in this island nation. In absence of any archaeological and similar other evidences, it is also not clear whether such trade link could be established to exploit the natural wealth of the country by the outside traders.

As in case of trade, prevalence of the myth, common in many respects in these countries are also not uniform. Transmission of myths, folk traditions is made only through interaction between people. As we have already seen that interaction of population of India in the form of traders with the neighbouring country of Sri Lanka, was in all respects greater, it is expected that myths prevalent in both these countries would be of common origin.

Table - 2 : Myth – Spread through interaction between people

	Trade link	Degree of interaction	Significance of mythical link
Sri Lanka	High degree of direct trade link	Interaction greater	Prevalence of myths of common origin significant
Nepal	Trade link with Tibet through Nepalese middle men at higher degree	Interaction greater	-do-
Bhutan	Trade link limited	Interaction	Insignificant presence of myths, comparatively less of common origin, probably due to non-availability of historical records.
Maldives	Insignificant trade link	Interaction minimum	Prevalence of mythical link insignificant, (only mythical stories of Koimala)

The above table tempts us to infer a close association of the traders and their accompanied people as carrier of all such myths. It may be argued that by this logic Nepal should also have similar myths since the people of this country had played a bridge role and maintained a close link with the trading communities of India. But it is not so. It seems quite a number of historical turmoil and upheaval that Nepal experienced resulted in the loss of records of such folk traditions. In case of Bhutan there was enough scope of such mythical stories as the country was very much linked with the Kamrupa State of India, but unfortunately no such myths are available so far. The reasons are difficult to ascertain since all documents related to the history of Bhutan got destroyed.

As in case of trade and myth, the extent of linkages through religion was also uneven. While Buddhism could spread firmly in Sri Lanka, it failed to do so in Nepal, though a number of *bhikhus* from India had paid several visits to this Himalayan country. The reason is not very difficult to understand. When King Ashoka took special interest towards preaching Buddhism in Sri Lanka, this island country had no other dominant religious faith which could resist Buddhism. Moreover, since the ruling royal family members accepted this religion and got themselves converted, the common people opted to follow them as a mark of their loyalty.

Acceptance of Buddhism by the common people was further expedited since preaching of this faith took place primarily with the help of language/dialects of the common people. The original canon was composed in a language different from Pali, though it became the lingua franca among the Buddhist monks of South Asian countries.

When Buddhism first entered in Nepal there was no dominant religion. Later on in the latter part of fourth century, Hinduism/Brahminism entered through a number of Hindu rulers. Subsequently Buddhism again entered this mountain nation through Padmasambhava. Because of the very tolerant ideological nature of Hinduism, it was not very difficult for Buddhism to make an inroad there. Though the rulers of

Table – 3 : Religion – Uneven spread of religion from India

	Agency	Followers	Preaching	Religion
SriLanka :				
(a) No dominant religion when Buddhism entered.	Royal family accepted Buddhism	Common people followed the rulers	Preaching was through local language/dialects	Hinayana Buddhism came from India
(b) Later on Hinduism (1st century B.C.) entered from Tamil country.	Tamil invaders ruled Sri Lanka for 27 years initially. Hinduism flourished. After some gap Tamils again ruled the country.	Common people followed the rulers	Buddhism and Hinduism coexisted	Buddhism lost much of its ground
Nepal : No dominant religion when Buddhism first entered (5th century B.C.). It was followed by spread of Hinduism	The royal family did not embrace Buddhism, but for the very tolerant nature of Hinduism, preaching of Buddhism was allowed.	A section of the people adopted Buddhism.	Preaching was through local language/dialects. Buddhism and Hinduism co-existed.	Mahayana Buddhism developed adopting local animism alongwith the Trantrik cult to suit the belief of local people.

Epilogue 141

(Brahmanism) through Hindu rulers of India. Padmasambhava successfully introduced Tantrik cult within the frame of Buddhism (8th century B.C.).		Mahayana Buddhism flourished through the Tibetan Buddhist.
Bhutan : Hinduism had existed when Buddhism entered.	The royal family accepted Buddhism.	Influx of Tibetan Buddhists outnumbered the Hindus.
Maldives : Buddhism reached much before Islamic faith spread in these islands. Influence of Hinduism evident from some customs and norms of the people of Gujarat.	—	Islamic invasion destroyed evidences of link through religion.

Nepal did not accept Buddhism as their religion, it could reach at certain levels among the common people because local language was used as means of communication for propagation of this religion. Buddhism, as a result, co-existed in Nepal along with Hinduism. Like in Nepal there were Hindu rulers in Bhutan also. Unlike Sri Lanka and Nepal Buddhism reached Bhutan when a Hindu king had invited Buddhist monk for his personal gain.

Mahayana Buddhism flourished in both Nepal and Bhutan, which reached these two countries from Tibet. While the people of Nepal had direct frequent interactions with those of Tibet for trading, the Nepalese had to frequently interact directly with the Buddhist population of Tibet for trade. To maintain the trade link uninterrupted, acceptance of the religion of the Tibetan traders is not very surprising. As a result Mahayana Buddhism could enter among a section of the people of Nepal. In case of Bhutan there was migration of Buddhist population in phases from Tibet to Bhutan. The Mahayana Buddhism that evolved in Tibet drew many elements from the existing Bon religion of that country. A compromise between some elements of Buddhism and Bon religion was thought to be very much convenient for acceptance of Buddhism to the commoners. As a result the people of Nepal and Bhutan did not put perceptible resistance to accept Mahayana Buddhism as their religion.

The present review thus brings into relief an important and hitherto untraversed area of research, namely the processes of peopling, cultural contact with its variable impact and biological relationship of the populations of the SAARC countries. But due to lack of information this could only be partially attended. This calls for generation of bio-cultural data on the population of all concerned countries in order to project a comprehensive profile of their bio-cultural affinities.

References

Agar, W.T., "Nepali Blood Groups", *Nature* 157, 1946, p. 270.

Agarwal, H.N., "Blood Groups of the Pasi with Special Reference to Their Genetic Relationship with Other Caste of Uttar Pradesh", *East Anthrop*, 15, 1962, pp. 161-4.

Agarwala, S.S., J.K. Sharma and J.E. Farooqi, "Study of G-6-PD Deficiency by BCB Dye Test in North Indians", *Human Population Genetics in India*, ed. by L.D. Sanghvi et al, Orient Longman, Bombay, 1974.

Allchin, B., "Palaeolithic Sites in the Plains of Sindh and Their Geographical Implications", *Geographical Journal*, 142 (3), Royal Society, London, 1976, pp. 472-89.

Allchin, F.R., "The Archaeology of Early Historic South Asia: The Emergence of Cities and States", Cambridge University Press, Cambridge, 1995.

Anand, J.P., "The Maldives: A Profile", *Encyclopaedia of the SAARC Nations*, Maldives, 1997, pp. 29-44.

Attabudin (cited in), "The Blood Groups in Pakistan" by W.C. Boyd and L.G. Boyd, *American Journal of Physical Anthropology*, 12, 1954, pp. 393-405

Banerjee, R.D., *Banglar Itihas* (Bengali), Gurudas Chattopadhayay & Sons, Calcutta, 1321, (Bengal Sambat).

Banerjee, Subrata, "Bangladesh", National Book Trust of India, New Delhi, 1981.

Basham, A.L. (ed), "A Cultural History of India", Oxford Press, Clarendon, 1975.

Bell, H.C.P., "Note on the Maldives Numerals", *Journal of the Royal Asiatic Society*, Ceylon Branch 7, p. 3, 1882.

— "The Maldives Islands: An Account of the Physical Features, Climate, History, Inhabitants, Production and Trade", Government Printers, Colombo, 1883.

— "The Maldives Islands: Monographs on the History, Archaeology and Epigraphy", Govt. Press, Colombo, 1940.

Bhalla, V., "Aspects of Gene Geography and Ethnic Diversity of the People of India", *Ethnicity, Caste and People*, ed. by K.S. Singh, Anthropological Survey of India, Calcutta, 1989.

Bhattacharya, Dilip, "Bhutan" (Bengali), Pharma K.L.M., Calcutta, 1981.

Bhattacharya, K.K. and S.K. Biswas, "Select Genetic Markers in Lakshadwip", *Man in India*, 58, 1978, pp. 65-70

Bhattacharjee, P.N., "Blood Group Investigations in the Abor Tribe", *Bulletin Department of Anthropology*, Govt. of India, 3 (1), 1954, pp. 51-4.

— "A Study on ABO Blood Groups and the ABH Secretion in the Nocte of North-East Frontier Agency", *Bulletin Department of Anthropology*, Govt. of India, 6 (1), 1957, pp. 77-80

Bhasin M.K., "The Blood Groups of the Newars of Nepal", *Human Biology*, 42, 1970, pp. 369-376

Bird, G.W.G., T.K. Jayaram, E.W. Ikin, A.E. Mourant and H. Lehmann, "The Blood Groups and the Haemoglobin of the Gorkha of Nepal", *American Journal of Physical Anthropology*, 15, pp. 163-169, 1957.

References

Bowels, G.T., "The People of Asia", Weidenfeld and Nicolson, London, 1977.

Brown, Percy, "The Borderland of Nepal", Archives Books, New Delhi, 1989.

Caplan, L., "Land and Social Change in East Nepal : A Study of Hindu Tribal Relations", University of California Press, Berkeley, 1970.

Cavilli – Sforza, L.L., P. Menozzi and P. Piazza, "The History and Geography of Human Genes", Princeton University Press, Princeton, 1994.

"Census of Sri Lanka", *Sri Lankan Year Book* (1981), Department of Census and Statistics (cited from Grover, 1997), Colombo, Sri Lanka, 1981.

Chakrabarti, B., "A Cultural History of Bhutan" Vol. I, Hilltop Publishers, Chittaranjan, 1979.

— "A Cultural History of Bhutan", Vol. II, Hilltop Publishers, Chittaranjan, 1980.

Chakraborti, D.K., "Ancient Bangladesh : A Study of Archaeological Sources", Oxford University Press, Delhi, 1992.

Chanda, R.P., "Indo-Aryan Races", *Indian Studies : Past & Present*, Calcutta, 1961.

Chattrjee, S.K., "Race Movements and Prehistoric Culture", *History and Culture of the Indian People*, ed. by R.C. Majumdar, London, 1952.

Chaudhuri, Mamata, "Shipbuilding in Ancient and Medieval India", *The Cultural Heritage of India,* Vol. VI, ed. by Priyadaranjan Ray and S.N. Sen, The Ramkrishna Mission Institute of Culture, Calcutta, 1986.

Chemjong, Iman Singh, "Kirat ko Veda" (Hindi) *History and Culture of the Kirat People, Nepal,* ed. by Rajendra Ram, Bihar, 1961.

Choudhury, B.N., "Bouddha Sahitya" (Bengali), Mahabodhi Book Agency, Calcutta, 1995.

Coelho, V. H., "History of Maldives – Sri Lanka Relations", *Encyclopaedia of the SAARC Nations*, Colombo-Maldives, 1997, pp. 45-64.

Cook, E.K., "Ceylon, its Geography, its Resources and its People", Macmillan & Co Ltd., London, 1951.

Corvinus, Gudrun, "The Prehistory of Nepal" (Theme Paper). *The Neogene and the Quaternary*, World Archaeological Congress, New Delhi, 1994.

Cottrell, L., "Concise Encyclopaedia of Archaeology", ed. by Hutchinson, London, 1960.

Dani, A.H., "Sanghao Cave Excavation, The First Season 1963", *Ancient Pakistan: Bulletin of the Department of Archaeology University of Peswar*, (Cited in Dani, 1988), 1964, p. 1.

Das, B.M., "ABO Blood Groups in the Tribal Populations of North East India with Special Reference to the Khasi", *Anthropologist*, Special Volume, 1969, pp. 85-92.

Das, S.R., D.P. Mukherjee and P.N. Bhattacharya, "Survey of the Blood Groups and PTC Test Among the Rajbanshi Caste of West Bengal (ABO, MNS, Rh, Duffy and Diago)", *Acta. Gentica Statistica Medica*, 17, 1967, pp. 433-45.

De, S.C., "Historicity of Ramayana and the Indo-Aryan Society in India and Ceylon", Ajanta Publications, Delhi, 1976.

Delson, E., "Ancestors: The Hard Evidence", (Cited in S.W. Kulatilake, Cranial Variation and Dispersal of Modern Humans in South Asia, Allan R. Liss. Inc., New York, 1996) 1985.

Denham, E.B., "The Races of Ceylon", *Ceylon at the Census of 1911*, (Cited in Maloney, 1980), Colombo, 1912.

Deraniyagala, S.U., "Prehistory of Sri Lanka" (Part-I & II) (cited in Kulatilake, 1996), Department of Archaeological Survey, Sri Lanka, 1992.

— "Pre and Protohistoric Settlement in Sri Lanka", *Economic Review*, Oct./Nov., 1997, pp.3-8.

De Silva, C.R., "Sri Lanka : A History", Vikas Publishing House Pvt. Ltd., New Delhi, 1987.

De Silva, K.M., "A History of Sri Lanka", Oxford University Press, Delhi, 1981.

Dev, Arabinda, "India and Bhutan: A Study in Frontier Political Relations (1772-1865)", Firma KLM Pvt. Ltd., Calcutta, 1976.

Dhavalikar, M.K., "Cultural Imperialism (Indus Civilisation in Western India)", Books and Books, New Delhi, 1995.

Dorji, C.T., Sonam Topgay, and Dorji Wangchuk, "Traditional Systems of Trans-Himalayan Flow of Goods and Services and Roles of Institutions Like Monasteries, Rituals, Friendship Among Trade Partners, Cultural Syncretism Facilitating Trans-Country Communication", Abstract, *Friendship Himalaya*, Indira Gandhi Rashtriya Manav Sangrahalaya, Bhopal, 1998.

Eliade, Mircea, "The Encyclopedia of Religion", Vol. 13, Macmillan, New York, 1987.

Embree, A.T., "Encyclopedia of Asian History" Vol.–1, Macmillan London, 1988.

— "Encyclopedia of Asian History", Vol–3, Macmillan, New York, 1988.

Foote, Robert Bruce, "Indian Prehistoric and Proto-historic Antiquity", Govt. Press, Madras, 1916.

Gaize, Frederick. H., "Regionalism and National Unity in Nepal", Vikas Publishing House Pvt. Ltd., Delhi, 1975.

Grover, Verinder (ed.), "Encyclopaedia of SAARC Nations: Bangladesh", Deep & Deep Publication, New Delhi, 1997.

— "Encyclopaedia of SAARC Nations: Bhutan", Deep & Deep Publication, New Delhi, 1997.

— "Encyclopaedia of the SAARC Nations: Pakistan", Deep & Deep Publication, New Delhi, 1997.

— "Encyclopaedia of SAARC Nations: Maldives", Deep & Deep Publication, New Delhi, 1997.

— "Encyclopaedia of SAARC Nations: Sri Lanka", Deep & Deep Publication, New Delhi, 1997.

Guha, B.S., "The Racial Affinities of the People of India", *Census of India*, 1931. Govt. of India, Simla, 1935.

— "Racial Elements in the Population", Oxford University Press, Bombay, 1944.

Ganguly, J.B., "The Modus Operandi of Trade Flow Between the Eastern Himalayan Sub-region and Assam in the Pre-colonial Period", (Abstract) *Friendship Himalaya*, Indira Gandhi Rashtriya Manav Sanghrahalaya, Bhopal, 1998.

Gautam, Rajesh and Ashoke K. Thapa Magar, "Tribal Ethnography of Nepal" Vol.-I, Book Faith India, Delhi, 1994.

— "Tribal Ethnography of Nepal" Vol.-II, Book Faith India, Delhi, 1994.

Ghurey, G.S., "Caste and Race in India", Popular Prakashan, Bombay, 1923.

Glasgow, B.G., M.J. Goodwine, F. Jackson, A.C. Kpec. H. Lehmann, A.E. Mourant. D. Tills, R.W.D. Turner and

M.P. Ward, "Blood Groups, Serum Groups and Haemoglobins of the Inhabitatnts of Lunana and Thimpu", *Vox. Sang* 14, Bhutan, 1968, pp. 31-42.

Gupta, M.B., "Sinhaler Shilpa O Sabhyata" (Bengali), Visva Bharati Granthalaya, Calcutta, 1953.

Harle, J.C., "The Art and Architecture of the Indian Subcontinent", Penguin Books, London, 1986.

Hulugalle, H.A.J., "Ceylon", Oxford University Press, London, 1946.

Hodgson, B.H., "On the Aborigines of the Sub-Himalayas", *Journal of Asiatic Society of Bengal*, 16, 1847, pp. 1235-1244.

Horrobin, D.F.J., S. Blackburne, E.W. Ikin, A.E. Mourant, J.P. Garlick and T. Cleghorn, "The Blood Groups of Some Nepalese Populations" (unpublished), (Cited from Mourant et al. 1976), 1966.

Jagadiswaran, "Calcutta Review", (*Cited from Brihat Banga, D.C. Sen*, 1941), University Press, Calcutta, 1933.

Joshi, B.L. and L.E. Rose, "Democratic Innovations in Nepal", University of California Press, Barkeley, 1966.

Kalla, A.K., "The Ethnology of India, Antecedents and Ethnic Affinities of People of India", Munsiram Manoharlal Publishers Pvt. Ltd., New Delhi, 1994.

Kalra, S.L., "Blood Groups of Punjabis and Maldivians", *Current Science*, 16, 1947, p. 92.

Karan, Pradyumma, P. and M. Jenkins William, "The Himalayan Kingdoms: Bhutan, Sikkim and Nepal", Van Nostrand, Princeton, 1963.

Kate, S.L., G.S. Mutalik, M.S. Phadke, V.A. Khedkar and M.N. Shende, "Prevalence of Erythrocyte, G-6-PD Deficiency in a Population of Poona District", *A Survey* in *Human Population Genetics in India*, ed. by Sanghvi et al. Orient Longman, Bombay, 1974.

Keith, Arther, "Racial Affinities of People of India", Census of India, 1931, Vol-1, pt. 3 Govt. of India, 1936.

Kennedy, K.A.R., "Biological Anthropology of Prehistoric South Asia", *The Anthropologist* 17 (1 & 2), 1970, pp. 1-13.

— "Biological Adaptations and Affinities of Mesolithic South Asia", *The People of S.E. Asia*, ed. by R. Luckas, 1984, pp. 29-57.

Kennedy, K.A.R., S.U. Deraniyagala, W.J. Rovertgen, J. Chinent and T. Disotell, "Upper Pleistocene Fossil Hominids from Sri Lanka", *American Journal of Physical Anthropology*, 72, 1987, pp. 441-461.

Kennedy, K.A.R. and S.U. Deraniyagala, "Fossil Remains of 28,000 – Year Old Hominids from Sri Lanka", (*Current Anthropology* 30, 1989, pp.394-399.

Kirk, K.L., "The Legend of Prince Vijaya: A Study of Sinhalese Origin", (*American Journal of Physical Anthropology*, 45, 1976 pp. 91-100.

Kirk, R.L., "Serum Protein and Enzyme Markers as Indicates of Population Affinities in Australian and the Western Pacific", *The Origin of the Australians*, ed. by R.L. Kirk and A.G. Thorne, Australian Institute of Aboriginal Studies, Canberra, 1976.

Kirk, R.L., L.Y.C. Lai, G.H. Vos, R.L. Wickremasinghe and D.J.B. Perera, "The Blood and Serum Group of Selected Population of South India and Ceylon", (*American Journal of Physical Anthropology* 20, 1962, pp. 485-97.

Kshatriya, G.K., "Genetic Affinities of Sri Lankan Populations", *Human Biology* 67 (b), 1995, pp. 843: 866.

References

Kulatilake, S.W., "Cranial Variation and the Dispersal of Modern Humans in South Asia", Tharanjee Prints, Sri Lanka, 1996.

Kumar, N., "Blood Group and Secretor Frequency Among the Galong", *Bulletin Department of Anthropology*, India 3 (1), 1954, pp. 55-65.

Kumar, N and D.B. Sastry, "A Genetic Survey Among the Riang: A Mongoloid Tribe of Tripura (North east India)", *Zeitscrift for Morphology and Anthropology* 51, 1961, pp. 346-55.

Lahr, M.M. and R.A. Foly, "Multiple Dispersals and Modern Human Origins", *Evolutionary Anthrppology*, 3, 1994, pp. 48-60.

Landon, Perceval, *Nepal* (Reprint 1993), Asian Educational Services, New Delhi, 1976.

Law, B.C. (Reprint)., "On the Chronicles of Ceylon", Asian Educational Services, New Delhi, 1994.

Leshink, L.S., "South Indian 'Megalithic Burials': The Pandukal Complex", Wies baden. F. Steiner, 1974.

Lukacs, J.R., "The People of South Asia: The Biological Anthropology of India, Pakistan and Nepal", Plenum Press, New York and London, 1984.

Madaan, D.K., "Maldives and SAARC: Economic and Trade Development", *Encyclopaedia of SAARC Nations, Vol. 7*, ed. by V. Grover, Maldives, 1997.

Mahalanobis, P.C., D.N. Majumdar and C.R. Rao, "Anthropometric Survey of the United Provinces: A Statistical Study", *Sankhya*, 9, 1949, pp. 98-324.

Majumdar, D.N., "ABO Blood Among the Garos of Eastern Pakistan", *Man in India* 3 (I), 1950, pp. 32-35.

Majumdar, D.N. and C.R. Rao, "Race Elements in Bengal", Asia Publishing House, Calcutta, 1960.

Majumdar R.C., "Ancient India", Motilal Banarasidass, Delhi, 1952.

— "The History and Culture of the Indian People: The Classical Age" (ed.), Bharatiya Vidya Bhavan, Bombay, 1954.

— "Hindu Colonies in the Far East", Firma K.L. Mokhopadhyay, Calcutta, 1963.

Majumdar, R.C., H.C. Raychaudhuri and Kalikinkar Datta, "An Advanced History of India", Macmillan & Co. Ltd., London, 1963.

Maloney, C., "People of the Maldives Islands", Orient Longman, Calcutta, 1980.

Masson–Oursell, P., H.W. Grabowska and P. Stern, Ancient India and Indian Civilisation, Lakshmi Book Store, New Delhi, 1967.

McCurdy, P.R. and L. Mahmood, "Red Cell Glucose-6 Phosphate Deficiency in Pakistan", *J.Lab. Clin. Med.* 76, (Cited in Mourant et al. 1976), 1970, pp. 943-48.

Mehra, G.N., "Bhutan: Land of the Peaceful Dragon", Vikas Publishing House Pvt. Ltd., Delhi, 1974.

Miki, T.T. Tanaka and T. Furuhata, "On the Distribution of ABO Blood Groups and the Taste Ability for Phenylthiocarbomide (P.T.C.) of the Lepcha and the Khasis", (*Proceedings of Japan Academy.* 36), 1960, pp. 78-80.

Mishra, S., "Prehistoric and Quarternary Studies at Nevasa: The Last 40 Years", *Quarternary Environments and Geo-archaeology of India* ed. by S. Wadia, R. Korisettar and V.S. Kale, Geological Survey of India, Bangalore, 1995.

Mourant et al., "The ABO Blood Groups", Black Well Publishers, Oxford, 1958.

Mourant, A.E., "Notes on Blood Groups in India", *Indian Anthropology*, ed. by T.N. Madan and G. Saran, Asia Publishing House, Bombay, 1962.

Mourant, A.E., A.C. Kopec and K.D. Sobezak, "The Distribution of the Human Blood Groups and Other Polymorphisms", Oxford University Press, London, 1976.

Mourant, A.E., M.J. Goodwine, A.C. Kopec., H.Lehmann, P.R. Steel and D. Tills, "The Hereditary Blood Factors of Some Population in Bhutan", *Anthropologist Special* Vol.-5, 1969, pp. 29-43.

Mukerjee, Radhakamal, "The Culture and Art of India", (first published, 1959), Munshiram Manoharlal Publishers Pvt.Ltd., 1984.

Nag, B. C., "Big Power Rivalry in Maldives", *Encyclopaedia of SAARC Nations*, Maldives, 1997.

Nakane, C., "A Plural Society in Sikkim: A Study of the Interrelationship of Lepcha, Bhotias and Nepalese", *Caste and Kin in Nepal, India and Ceylon*, Asia, New York, 1966.

Nepali, Gopal Singh, "The Newars", United Asia Publications, Bombay, 1965.

Northey, W. Brook and Morris, C.J., "The Gurkhas", Cosmo Publication, New Delhi, 1974.

Nuri, M.H., "Maldives in the 1990's "*Encyclopaedia of SAARC Nations*", Vol.-7, ed. by V. Grover, Maldives, 1997.

Obeyeskere, Gananath, "The Cult of teh Goddess Pattini", The University of Chicago Press, Chicago, 1984.

Papiha, S. et al., "Genetic Variation in Sri Lanka", *Human Biology* 68 (5), 1996, pp. 707-737.

Pemble, John, "The Invasion of Nepal", Clarendon Press, Oxford, 1971.

Pillai, K.K., "South India and Ceylon", (cited from Maloney 1980), University of Madras 1963.

Qureshi, I.H., "Pakistan. Lands and People", *The World Facts and Figure Index* Vol. 2, Grolier, New York, 1976, p.157.

Ram, Rahul, "Modern Bhutan", Vikas Publications, Delhi, 1971.

Rapson, E.J., "Ancient India", (Reprint), Susil Gupta (India) Ltd., Calcutta, 1960.

Rapson, E.J. (ed.), "The Cambridge History of India Vol-I, Ancient India", S. Chand & Co., Delhi, 1955.

Ray, Priyadaranjan and S.N. Sen, "The Cultural Heritage of India" Vol. VI, The Ramakrishna Mission Institute of Culture, Calcutta, 1986.

Rashid, Er. Haroun, "Geography of Bangladesh: Dhaka", The University Press Ltd., 1977.

Regmi, D.R., "Modern Nepal", Firma K.L. Mukhopadhyay, Calcutta, 1975.

Reynolds, C.H.B., "Linguistic Strands in the Maldives", *Contributions to Asian Studies*, Clarence Maloney, E.J. Brill, Leiden, 1978.

Risley, Herbert, "The People of India", Thacker Spink & Co., Calcutta, 1915.

Rose, L.E., "The Politics of Bhutan", Cornell University Press, Ithaca, 1977.

Rose, L.E. and M.W. Fisher, "The Politics of Nepal", Cornell University Press, London, 1970.

Roy, Chowdhury, H.C., "Physical and Historical Geography", *History of Bengal*, Vol. I, University of Dhaka, 1943.

Roberts, D.F., L.K. Creen and K.P. Abeyaratne, "Blood Groups of the Sinhalese", *Man*, 7 (I), 1972, pp. 122-127.

Roberts, D.F., S.S. Papiha and K.P. Abeyaratne, "Red Cell Enzyme Polymorphism in Ceylon Sinhalese", *American Journal of Human Genetics*, 24, 1972, pp. 181-188.

Ronald, A.R., B.A.Underwood and T.E. Woodward, "Underwood and Glucose Phosphate Dehydrogenase deficiency in Pakistani Males", *Transaction of Royal Society of Tropical Medicine and Hygiene*. 62, (Cited in Mourant et al. 1976), 1968, pp.531-33.

Roy, Choudhury, A.K., "Genetic Relationship Between Indian Populations and Their Neighbours", *The People of South Asia*, ed. by J.R. Lukacs, Plenum Press, New York and London, 1984.

Roy, Choudhury, A.K., "Genetic Polymorphism in Human Populations in India", *People of India, Some Genetical Aspects*, ed. by G.V. Satyavati ICME, New Delhi, 1983.

Roy Choudhury, A.K., M. Nei, "Human Polymorphic Genes: World Distribution", Oxford University Press, Oxford, 1988.

Roy, S.C., "Mundas and Their Country", City Book Society, Calcutta, 1912.

Saha, N., "Blood Genetic Markers in Sri Lanka Populations – Reappraisal of the Legend of Prince Vijaya", *American Journal of Physical Anthropology*, 76, 1988, pp. 217-225.

Saletore, R. N., "Encyclopaedia of Indian Culture", Vol. I, Sterling Publishers Pvt. Ltd., New Delhi, (Reprint 1986).

Sankalia, H.D., "Ramayana: Myth or Reality?", People's Publishing House, New Delhi, 1973.

Sanyal, B.D., "The People of Nepal", *Eastern Anthropologist* I (I), 1947-48, pp. 1-7.

Sanyal, Hitesranjan, "A Study of a Few Mangalkavya Text", *Occasional Paper* No. 52, Centre for Studies of Social Science, Calcutta, 1982.

Sastri, Nilkantha K.A., "Age of the Nandas and Mauryas", Motilal Banarasidass, Benaras, 1952.

Sarkar, S.S., "The Autochthons of India", *Man in India*, 33, 1953, p. 195.

Sarkar, S.S., "Ancient Races of Baluchistan, Punjab and Sind", Bookland Private Ltd., Calcutta, 1969.

Sarkar, S.S., "Ancient Races of Deccan", Munshiram Manoharlal, New Delhi, 1972.

Sen, D.C., "Brihat Banga" (Bengali), University Press, Calcutta, 1941.

Sen, Dinesh Chandra, "Brihat Banga" (Bengali) Vol. I, Dey's Publishing, Calcutta, 1993.

Sen, Sukumar (ed.), "Chandimangal" (Bengali), Sahitya Akademi, New Delhi, 1975.

Senaveratna, John M., "The Story of the Sinhalese", Asian Educational Services (AES Report), New Delhi, 1997.

Seneviratne, R.D., "The Archaeology of the Megalithic Black and Red Ware Complex of Sri Lanka", *Ancient Ceylon* 5, (cited from Kennedy and Deraniyagala, 1989.), 1984, pp. 237-307.

Singh, A.K., "Indo-Roman Trade", Janaki Prakashan, Patna, 1988.

Singh, Madanjeet, "Himalayan Art", New York Graphic Society Ltd., New York, 1968.

Singh, Munshi Shew Shunker and Pandit Sri Gunanand, "History of Nepal", Low Price Publications, Delhi (A Division of D.K. Publishers & Distributors (P) Ltd.), (Reprint 1995), 1877.

Singh, Nagendra, "Bhutan: A Kingdom in the Himalayas", Thomson Press (India) Ltd., New Delhi, 1972.

Sinha, A.C., "Politics of Sikkim: A Sociological Study", Thomson Press (India) Ltd., New Delhi, 1975.

References

— "Bhutan Ethnic Identity and National Dilemma", Reliance Publishing House, New Delhi, 1991.

Sinha, S.K., "Medieval History of the Deccan", Vol. I, Govt. of Andhra Pradesh, Hyderabad, 1964.

Simmons, R.T., "The Biological Origin of Australian Aboriginals", *The Origin of the Australians*, ed. by R.L.Kirk and A.G. Thorne, 1976.

Smith, V., "*A History of Fine Art in India and Ceylone : From the Earliest Times to the Present Day*, Clarendon Press, Oxford, 1911.

Srivastava, R.P., "Blood Groups in the Tharus of Uttar Pradesh and Their bearing on Ethnic and Genetic Relationships", *Human Biology*, 37, 1965, pp.1-42.

Stern, M.A., A.M.B., Pamela Kynoch and H. Lehmann, "Thalassaemia, G6PD Deficiency and Haemoglobin D-Punjab in Pathans", *Lancet*. I., 1968, pp. 1284-5.

Stiles, D., "Palaeolithic Artifacts in Siwalik and Post Siwalik Deposits of Northern Pakistan", *Kroeber, Anthropological Society Papers* nos. 53/54, 1978, pp. 129-48.

Subba, M.S. and B. Chettri, "Thakuri and Malla Kings of Nepal", *Munal*, Vol. 2 No. 8, 1998.

Subba, T.B., "Dynamics of a Hill Society: The Nepalis in Darjeeling and Sikkim Highland", Mittal Publications, Delhi, 1989.

Sur, Atul, "History and Culture of Bengal", Chakrabarti & Chatterjee Co., Calcutta, 1963.

Thapa, Netra B., "A Short History of Nepal", Ratna Pustak Bhandar, Kathmandu, 1981.

Tiwari, S.C., "Anthropmetric Study of the Bhotias of Almora", District. U.P. (*The Anthropologist* I), 1954, pp. 22-33.

Tresidder, A.J., "Ceylon – An Introduction to the 'Resplendent Land', D.V. Nostrand Company Inc., Princeton, Toronto, 1960.

Trotter, M., "Estimation of Stature from Intact Limb Bones", *Personal Identification in Mass Disasters, ed. by T.D. Steward*, National Museum of Natural History: Cited from Kennedy and Kennedy 1984), Washington D.C., 1970.

Vansittart, Eden, "Notes on Nepal", Asian Educational Services, New Delhi, 1992.

Varma, R.S. (ed.), "Cultural Heritage of Nepal", Kitab Mahal, Allahabad, 1972.

Walker, Benjamin, "Hindu World: An Enchyclopedic Survey of Hinduism" Vol. II., George Allen & Unwin Ltd., London, 1968.

Wheeler, R.E.M., "Five Thousand year of Pakistan – An Archaeological Outline", Christopher Johnson (Pub.) Ltd., London, 1950.

White, J.C., "Sikkim and Bhutan", Vivek Publishing House, Delhi, 1971.

Wickremasingh, R.L, E.W. Ikin, A.E. Mourant, "The Blood Groups and Haemoglobin of the Vedda of Ceylon", *Journal of Royal Anthropological Institute*, 93), 1963, pp. 117-125.

Wijayapala, W.H. (Cited in S.U. Deraniyagala 1997), 1992.

Wilhelm, Geiger, "Mahavansha", (Trans), Colombo, 1931.

Willis, J.C., "Ceylon: A Handbook for the Resident and the Traveller", Colombo Apothecaries Co., Peradeniya, 1907.

Willis, Roy (ed.), "Word Mythology", Simon & Schuster, London, 1993.

Worman, E.C., "The Neolithic Problem in the Prehistory of India", *Journal of the Washington Academy of Science*, 1949.

About the Contributors...

Dr. Jayanta Sarkar (b. 1943), M. Sc. (Gold Medal), Ph.D. (Ranchi) in Anthropology is attached with the Anthropological Survey of India as Deputy Director. He has more than 35 years of research experience in the field of Cultural Anthropology with special reference to social change among the tribal and non-tribal populations living in the different ecological settings in India. Conducted intensive field investigations in the Himalayan region of the northeastern India. Conducted intensive field investigations in the himalayan region of the northeastern India, tribal dominated areas of Madhya Pradesh and Chattishgarh, different caste and religious groups living in the industrial and urban settings of east and south India and also among the hunter and food gatherer tribes of the Andaman Islands.

Dr. Sarkar is the author/co-author/editor of a dozen books in English and three in Bengali and author of more than 50 anthropological papers published in India.

Dr. G.C. Ghosh (b. 1941), M.Sc., Ph.D. in Anthropology (Calcutta) was associated with the Anthropological Survey of India till his superannuation in 2001 as Deputy Director.

Dr. Ghosh has long-standing experience in the field of Anthropological research particularly in Physical Anthropology. He has carried out extensive field investigation among various castes, tribes and communities of different States and Union Territories. He was involved in most of the national projects of physical anthropology under taken by the Survey in various capacities, including project in charge/coordinator. His major areas of research contribution relate to dermatoglyphics, sro-anthropology, anthropometry, demography, indigenous health practices and nutritional anthropology. He has to his credit a number of scientific papers published in India and abroad and five books released by the Anthropological Survey of India.

Dr. Chumki Piplai (b. 1951), M.Sc., Ph.D. (Calcutta) is working as Research Associate in the Anthropological Survey of India. She has conducted fieldwork among the tea-garden labourers, various tribes, including the Jarawas of Andaman Islands, besides non-tribal communities of main land India. She has specialisation broadly in the study on human biological aspect. Dr. Piplai has several research papers to her credit published in India and abroad.

J.M. Sarkar (b. 1948), M.Sc. in Anthropology (Ranchi) has been conducting research in the field of Physical Anthropology, specially sero-genetics, morpho-genetics and demographic studies on the tribes and non-tribes of India. Presently working as a Research Associate (Physical) in the Anthropological Survey of India and has published a number of research papers.

Dr. Jyotirmoy Chakraborty (b. 1952), M.Sc. in Anthropology (Calcutta), Ph.D. (Sambalpur) has specialisation in Cultural Anthropology. He joined the Anthropological Survey of India in 1977. Dr. Chakraborty has completed several national and regional projects commissioned by the Anthropological Survey of India. He has carried out extensive field investigations in Rajasthan, Gujarat, West Bengal and Sikkim. His present interest in research are: Ethnicity, Culture change and Religious syncretism. He is a life member of many professional associations and societies. Dr. Chakraborty has to his credit a number of research papers published in India.

Rabiranjan Biswas (b. 1957), M.Sc. in Anthropology (Calcutta) joined in the Anthropological Survey of India in 1984. He has worked in the field of Cultural Anthropology on both tribal and non-tribal population of Uttar Pradesh and Orissa. His major areas of field studies are ethnicity and politics; structure and transformation in tribal societies and agrarian relation in India.